His arm snake he dragged h dropping to he

She'd never been k unlike her fiancé. Ov had changed. He was so muscular, so solid. How could this be? she wondered to herself.

The darkness was so intense she couldn't see his features, could only feel him, the unfamiliar hardness of his body. She tried to push him away, but he only deepened the kiss, holding her to him as if he never wanted to let her go, as if he'd been waiting for her, needing her. Suddenly he seemed so different....

She lost herself in his kiss, stirred by an intensity she'd never felt before at his unexpected ardor. It was as if they'd never touched before....

And then she knew.

He was someone else....

Dear Harlequin Intrigue Reader,

We've got some of your favorite Harlequin Intrigue authors heating up the book racks this month— *USA TODAY* bestselling author Susan Kearney among them. Susan concludes her action-packed HEROES INC. trilogy with an exciting story about *Saving the Girl Next Door*. And look for more HEROES INC. titles in the future from Harlequin Intrigue *and* Blaze.

Joanna Wayne pens another southern scorcher in her HIDDEN PASSIONS series. *Attempted Matrimony* explores the desperation of one woman who's married a madman...and how one good man's love for her is stronger than any evil.

Veteran Harlequin Intrigue author Caroline Burnes winds up THE LEGEND OF BLACKTHORN duo with *Babe in the Woods*. We know our readers love gothic stories, and you get a double dose of classic enchantment in this terrific companion series.

Finally, enjoy the allure of a true mystery lover in *The Masked Man* by B.J. Daniels

Sincerely,

Denise O'Sullivan
Senior Editor
Harlequin Intrigue

THE
MASKED MAN
B.J. DANIELS

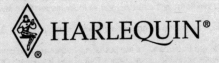

TORONTO • NEW YORK • LONDON
AMSTERDAM • PARIS • SYDNEY • HAMBURG
STOCKHOLM • ATHENS • TOKYO • MILAN • MADRID
PRAGUE • WARSAW • BUDAPEST • AUCKLAND

ISBN 0-373-22716-7

THE MASKED MAN

ABOUT THE AUTHOR

B.J. Daniels sets her latest book in the backwoods of Montana, a place she knows well. She's lived in Montana since she was five, when her family moved to a cabin her father built in the Gallatin Canyon.

A former award-winning journalist, B.J. had thirty-six short stories published before she wrote and sold her first romantic suspense, *Odd Man Out,* which was later nominated for the *Romantic Times* Reviewer's Choice Award for Best First Book and Best Harlequin Intrigue.

B.J. lives in Bozeman with her husband, Parker, two springer spaniels, Zoey and Scout, and an irascible tomcat named Jeff. She is a member of the Bozeman Writers Group and Romance Writers of America. To contact her, write: P.O. Box 183, Bozeman, MT 59771.

Books by B.J. Daniels

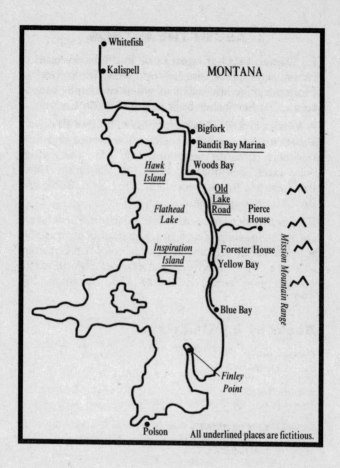

CAST OF CHARACTERS

Jill Lawson—The owner of The Best Buns in Town bakery expects her fiancé to be waiting for her in the dark cottage the night of the masquerade party. Instead, she finds a masked man who fulfills her fantasies—and makes her a suspect in a murder.

MacKenzie Cooper—The private investigator is lured into more than murder....

Trevor Forester—He wants it all, including Inspiration Island and Jill Lawson—and he has lied, cheated and stolen to get them. No wonder someone wants him dead.

Nathaniel Pierce—He has everything money can buy—and then some. But when his most prized possessions are stolen, he will do *anything* to get them back.

Heddy and Alistair Forester—They thought they were doing the right thing, raising their son Trevor to appreciate the finer things in life.

Rachel Wells—She was finally going to get what she deserved.

Shane Ramsey—Mac's nephew has always gotten into trouble, but this time he's in way over his head.

Arnie Evans—Trevor Forester's best friend did whatever Trevor told him to. Now he's paying the price.

This book is for Travis Ness,
who came into our lives on a prayer—
and now believes in love at first sight. Montana born,
he loves our annual summer weekend at Flathead Lake.
He also loves my daughter, and we love him.

Prologue

He picked her up in his headlights as he came around the curve. She stood beside the narrow lake road, thumb out. He slowed to make sure before he stopped, but his blood was already pounding.

Yes. Long blond hair, sun-kissed bare limbs, sixteen, seventeen tops. She wore a pink T-shirt that hugged her small breasts and navy shorts that exposed slim, coltish legs and, as he stopped the car beside her, he saw that she had The Look.

He was a sucker for The Look. That cool, confident conviction that her life was only just beginning, that she would live forever, that nothing would harm *her*. It was a look that came only with youth.

"Hey," he said as he rolled down the passenger-side window and leaned over to smile at her. "Where ya headed?"

She stepped closer, bending at the waist to look in at him. "Bigfork?"

Her sweet scent rushed in with the warm summer night. Raspberry, he thought, one of his favorites. She hooked a hand over the open window frame. Her fingernails were painted a pale pink. He really liked that. On her slim, tanned wrist a tiny silver charm bracelet with a perfect little silver heart tinkled softly.

He could hardly contain himself. "Hop in, I'm going that way. You must be in Bigfork working for the summer." He didn't want to make the mistake of trying to pick up a local girl again.

She nodded, stepped closer.

It always came down to a few crucial seconds.

She glanced at his car, then at him again.

In her blue eyes he saw that instant of uncertainty that could save—or destroy—her.

Seconds. Life or death. He loved this part.

"Thanks," she said and reached for the door handle. *Ain't no big, bad wolf here.*

He smiled. All teeth.

Chapter One

Jill Lawson couldn't believe it.

Trevor had stood her up *again*. Only this time it was for his parents' anniversary masquerade party. This time she was dressed as Scarlett O'Hara and feeling foolish as she waited in a far wing of the house, alone. This time was going to be the last time.

"I can't marry this man. I'm breaking off the engagement." The words echoed in the dark, empty room. *"Tonight."*

She watched the approaching thunderstorm move across the lake and waited for the aftershock of her decision. She had expected to feel something other than...relief. Certainly more regret.

She didn't.

This far down the east wing of the Foresters' massive lake house the sounds of the ongoing party were muted. That was one of the reasons she had come down here. To get away from all the merriment and the reminder that she was alone, the engagement ring on her finger feeling suddenly too tight. The ache in her heart too familiar.

She ached for something she wasn't even sure existed except maybe in the movies.

"You act like you expect fireworks, maybe the earth to move? Really, Jill, you are such a fool," Trevor had said when she'd tried to voice her concerns the last time she'd seen him.

Well, she certainly felt like a fool tonight, she thought. She had hardly seen Trevor since he'd asked her to marry him, but when he'd called, he'd promised that tonight would be different. After all, it was his parents' thirty-fifth anniversary, and summer was almost over, another season gone.

Heddy and Alistair threw a costume party to celebrate the event at the end of August every year at their house on the east shore of Flathead Lake. This year the theme was famous lovers, and Trevor had insisted Jill come as Scarlett so he could be Rhett Butler. And he'd stood her up.

"Quite frankly, Rhett, I don't give a damn," she said to the dark room. A lie. She did give a damn. She had wanted Trevor Forester to be The One. And at first, he'd made her believe he was.

She looked down at the silver charm bracelet on her wrist, the tiny heart dangling from the chain, and remembered the night he'd given it to her. On her birthday two months ago. It was right after that when he'd asked her to marry him and had given her the antique engagement ring now on her finger.

Her instincts warned her that everything between her and Trevor had happened too fast. She'd let him bowl her over, not giving her time to think. Or hardly react. And suddenly she was engaged to a man she didn't really know.

He'd been involved in his construction project, an upscale resort he called Inspiration Island south of Bigfork, Montana, in the middle of Flathead Lake, almost since they'd started dating.

Admittedly, he *had* been working a lot. A week ago he'd stopped by her bakery and she'd barely recognized him. He was tanned, leaner, more muscular.

She felt herself weaken a little at the memory of how good he'd looked and quickly was reminded that he had only made love to her once, soon after the engagement. In the weeks since, he always had an excuse—he was too tired or had to meet one of the investors or had to get back to the island.

"Everything will be different once we're married," he'd promised.

"Right," she said to the dark. She didn't believe that. Didn't believe anything Trevor told her anymore. "We're never going to know if things will be different because I'm not marrying you, Trevor Forester." She spun around in surprise. Someone had come into the dark room without her realizing it. How long had he or she been there, listening?

A small table lamp came on, blinding her for an instant. She thought at first the other person was Trevor and she would get this over with quickly. This quiet wing of the house would serve her purpose well.

But it wasn't Trevor. "I heard you mention my son's name," Heddy Forester said. She was dressed as Cleopatra. Her Anthony, Alistair Forester, didn't seem to be with her.

Obviously Heddy had heard her. But Jill didn't want to spoil Heddy's anniversary party. The older woman would hear soon enough about the broken engagement. Then again, maybe Heddy wouldn't be that disappointed by the news.

"I'm just upset because Trevor is so late," Jill said.

"I'm sure he has a good reason." Heddy always defended her only offspring. "He's been working such long hours on the island."

"Yes, but I thought he'd call," Jill said, trying not to show just how upset she really was. Heddy Forester didn't miss much, though.

"Maybe he can't get to a phone," Heddy offered, studying her. The sound of music, chattering guests and fireworks going off drifted in from the patio. There must have been at least a hundred people at the party.

Jill thought about mentioning that Trevor had a cell phone with him all the time, but didn't. "I'm sure he'll be along soon," she said diplomatically. In the distance thunder rumbled, the horizon over the lake dark and ominous.

"Or maybe he's trapped on the island and can't get back," Heddy suggested, looking anxiously out the window at the storm brewing over the water. "I'll bet his cell phone won't work in a storm like this."

"I thought Trevor wasn't going to the island to-day."

Heddy didn't seem to hear. "I'd better get my guests in before the storm hits. Send Trevor to find me when he arrives."

Jill nodded. Heddy was right. Trevor wouldn't miss his parents' anniversary party. He had to have a good reason for being this late. For standing Jill up. Again.

After Heddy left, Jill turned the light back off, preferring to watch the approaching storm in the dark, preferring to let Trevor find her. She loved thunderstorms, the dramatic light, the awesome power, the smell of the rain-washed summer evening afterward.

She didn't know how long she stood there, watching all the guests rush in as the storm moved across the water toward them, the darkness complete. Down the slope from the house, the wind tore leaves from the trees and sent waves splashing over the docks. Jill caught the flicker of boat lights on the other side of the Foresters' small guest cottage at the edge of the lake and wondered what fool would go out in a storm like this.

Speaking of fools... She glanced at her watch. Eight-fifteen. Trevor was almost two hours late. Thunder rumbled in the distance. The red-white-and-blue flags snapped in the wind out on the patio under a flapping striped canopy. The patio was empty, everyone now inside as lightning flashed and thunder rumbled. She should go home before it started to rain.

She could break off the engagement tomorrow. Tomorrow, when she was less angry. Tomorrow, when she wasn't dressed in a hoop skirt and green-velvet curtain material. Why had Trevor insisted they come to the party as Rhett Butler and Scarlett O'Hara, anyway? Hadn't Scarlett ended up alone?

Then again, maybe this was the perfect costume.

"Say good-night, Scarlett," she said to the room and started to turn from the window. A jagged bolt of lightning flashed, spiking down into the water, illuminating the patio and the curve of rock steps that swept down the grassy slope to the lake cottage. And in that flash of light she saw him.

Rhett Butler. He ducked into the cottage just an instant before thunder rumbled overhead. The first raindrops spattered the window. Trevor must have been on the boat she'd seen and now he'd gone into the cottage to wait out the storm.

When the lights didn't come on inside the cottage, she realized the shutters were closed. Trevor was alone down there, offering her the perfect opportunity to talk to him. This couldn't wait. She suspected he'd been avoiding her because he, too, thought their engagement was a mistake. He couldn't avoid her now.

She braced herself, then opened the patio door, lifted the hoop skirt with one hand and, holding on to her hat with the other, raced across the patio to the rock steps that descended to the cottage.

Behind her, the wind moaned through the trees, sending leaves scurrying. Snatches of the music from the party chased after her but were quickly drowned out by the crash of waves. Lightning struck so close it raised the tiny hairs on the back of her neck. As she ran toward the cottage, rain slashed down, hard as hail and just as cold. Thunder boomed, deafening.

She was close enough to the water now that she could feel the spray from the waves. Her hand was on the doorknob when lightning electrified the sky overhead once more. This time the thunderclap reverberated in her chest.

The lights on the patio blinked out and behind her the main house went dark. She opened the cottage door, the room inside as black as the bottom of a bucket. Chilled, wet and a little disoriented by the darkness, she stepped in and quickly closed the door behind her.

Her lips parted as she started to say Trevor's name, sensing, rather than hearing, him near her.

Before she could get his name out, his arm snaked around her waist and he dragged her to him, his mouth unerringly dropping to hers.

She gasped in surprise and pushed with both palms against his broad chest, the darkness so intense she couldn't see his features, could only feel him, the unfamiliar Rhett Butler costume mustache, the unfamiliar hardness of his body. Had he seen her coming down from the house and thought he could make things up to her by taking her to bed? Fat chance.

She tried to push him away, but he only deepened the kiss, holding her to him as if he never wanted to let her go, as if he'd been waiting for her, needing her.

This wasn't why she'd come down here. Or was

it? Had she secretly hoped Trevor could change her mind?

He groaned against her mouth and she felt herself weaken in his arms. He'd never kissed her like this before. His body was so muscular, so solid, harder than it had been the last time they'd made love.

If this was his way of saying he was sorry… She lost herself in his kiss, in the warmth of his body molded to hers, stirred in a way she'd never been before by this unexpected ardor.

Her hat fell to the floor as he buried his fingers in her hair and pressed her against the wall with his body, his mouth exploring hers as his hand moved up her waist and over her rib cage to cup her breast in his warm palm. Heat shot through her.

She had never wanted him so badly. Her body felt on fire as he moved his hands over her, exploring her flesh with his fingertips in the blind darkness. She arched against him, strangely uninhibited. There was something exciting about not being able to see each other, only feel. It was as if they'd never touched before as his fingers explored beneath the confines of her costume.

His touch sure and strong, he swiftly and efficiently relieved her of her clothing, the hoop skirt, the entire dress, leaving only her skimpy silk panties and bra.

Outside the warm cottage the storm raged. She sighed with pleasure against his mouth, his lips never leaving hers as if he'd feared what she might have said if he hadn't kissed her the moment she came into the cottage. Had he realized how abandoned and alone she'd been feeling? How afraid she was that they were about to make a mistake by marrying?

She'd never felt more naked as his fingers skimmed over her skin, stopping to fondle her through the thin silk of her underthings. Hadn't she, in fact, worn the sexy lingerie hoping things would be different between them tonight, just as Trevor had promised?

She worked feverishly at the buttons of his costume, his kisses growing more ardent, more demanding, her need becoming more frantic as she worked with wanton abandon to free him of his clothing. His need matched hers as he relieved her of her bra and panties and helped discard his own clothing, and all the time, never stopped kissing her.

She shuddered at the first touch of his naked skin against hers, heard his soft groan as he dragged her down to the floor, their lovemaking as wild and frenzied as the storm outside.

He took her higher than she'd ever been, a rarefied place depleted of oxygen, where stars blinded her vision and each breath seemed her last until the final crescendo of storm and passion and release, sending her reeling into a dark, infinite universe of pleasure.

She felt tears come to her eyes as he curled her to him on the floor, spooning her into his warmth, spent and seemingly as awed as she.

She snuggled close, content for the first time in her life. She knew there was no going back. She'd just committed to this man in a way more binding

than any engagement ring or pronouncement of
love. She'd been so wrong about him. So wrong
about *them.*

She closed her eyes, her skin still tingling, her
heart still hammering like the rain on the roof. She
didn't hear the door open.

A chill wind blew in, rippling over her skin. At
the same moment she opened her eyes, a flash of
lightning lit the outside world, illuminating the driving rain—and the dark figure silhouetted in the doorway.

So content, so sated, so happy was Jill that it took
her a moment to recognize the familiar silhouette in
the doorway. The hat, the hair, the hoop skirt. Another Scarlett. It took even longer for the words the
other Scarlett spoke to register. "Trevor, darling,
I'm sorry I'm late but I—"

In that instant Jill saw the other Scarlett take in
the hurriedly discarded costumes on the floor, her
head coming up to look where Jill lay on the floor
in Trevor's arms in that instant before the lightning
flash blinked out, pitching everything back into
blackness.

"You bastard!" the woman shrieked. "You
lousy—" A boom of thunder drowned out the rest
as she whirled away.

For just an instant Jill didn't move. Then the truth
hit her. A cry caught in her throat as she jerked free
of Trevor's arms, recoiling in shame. She stumbled
to her feet and grabbed at the pile of clothing she'd
seen in that flash of light, that flash of understanding—Trevor had thought he was making love to

someone else! The other Scarlett. No wonder it had been so passionate! So amazingly tender and loving and filled with desire!

Behind her, he still hadn't said a word. But she could feel him watching her. Wasn't he even going to bother to try to talk himself out of this?

It was too dark inside the cottage to find her skimpy underwear. With her back to him, she dressed with only one thing in mind—getting out of there as quickly as possible. She pulled on the hoop, frantically tied it and slipped the damp dress over her head, then felt around for her shoes in the dark, wanting nothing more than to flee before he tried to apologize, which would make it all so much worse.

On the way to the door she tripped on her hat, which she then swept up from the floor. Fighting tears of humiliation and anger, she tugged off the engagement ring.

She was grateful for the darkness in the cottage. From the doorway she didn't have to see his face, only the dark shape of him on the floor. He hadn't moved. Hadn't said a word. But then, what could he say?

"You *are* a lousy bastard, Trevor Forester," she said, and flung the engagement ring at him before rushing out.

Fool that she was, she expected to hear him call after her. She thought she heard him groan, but it could have been the wind.

She lifted the wet velvet hem of the dress and, her shoes still in her hand, ran up the hillside, avoiding the main house, afraid to look back for fear she would see Trevor standing in the doorway of the cottage—and feel something other than hatred for him.

She didn't let herself cry until she was in her van driving back to her apartment over the bakery. Tears scalded her eyes, blurring her vision as the windshield wipers clacked back and forth against the pounding rain.

She could still smell him on her, still feel his touch as if it was imprinted on her skin, still taste his kisses. Damn Trevor Forester. Damn him to hell.

Rain fell in a torrent. Jill barely recognized the little red Saturn sedan that almost ran her off the road as it came up from behind and whizzed past, going too fast for the narrow, winding road along the lakeshore. But in her headlights she read the personalized license plate: JILLS. It was her car, the car Trevor had borrowed the last time she'd seen him, saying his Audi Quatro sports car was in the shop. Since then, Jill had been driving her bakery delivery van with The Best Buns In Town painted on the side.

The driver went by so fast that Jill hadn't seen who was behind the wheel. Trevor? Or had he loaned her car to his girlfriend? Or were they both in the car?

And Jill thought she was angry with Trevor before!

She pushed the van's gas pedal of the van to the floor, trying to close the distance between her and the red Saturn. Was Trevor hoping to beat her back to her apartment? Beg her forgiveness? Or trying to get away? He had to have recognized the van. It was darned hard to miss.

Jill kept the Saturn's taillights in sight as she raced after it, the van forced to take the curves more slowly. The narrow road was cut into the side of the mountain. In some places, the land beneath the road dropped in rocky cliffs to the water. In others, cherry orchards clung to the steep hillside for miles, broken only by tall dense pines and rock.

On the outskirts of Bigfork, Montana, the Saturn turned right into a new complex, where Trevor had rented a condo until he and Jill were married. At least that had been the plan. He had said he was going to buy her a house on the lake. He didn't want them living in some dinky condo.

As Jill parked the van behind her car in front of the condo, she told herself she should just take the car and leave. As angry as she was, this wouldn't be a good time for a confrontation—with Trevor or his girlfriend.

But then, how would she get the van back to the bakery? She'd need it early in the morning to make deliveries.

Also, she would never know who'd been driving her car. And suddenly she had a whole lot she wanted to say to Trevor. Or his girlfriend. Or both.

She got out of the van in the cumbersome costume. The front door of the condo stood open, a faint light on inside. Whoever had gone in must have been in a big hurry.

It was dark inside the condo. She could hear what sounded like someone rummaging around in the bedroom. The only light spilled from the partially opened bedroom doorway. From this angle, Jill could see nothing but shadowed movement on one wall and the flicker of what had to be a flashlight beam.

Her heart caught in her throat. Why hadn't the person in the bedroom turned on the lights? And why would Trevor be searching for something in his own bedroom in the dark?

The other Scarlett?

Jill moved through the dark living room following the path of light coming from the bedroom and caught the scent of the woman's perfume. She realized she'd smelled it earlier—that moment when the other Scarlett had been framed in the lake cottage doorway. A heavy, cloying scent that made her sick to her stomach.

Trevor had never been much of a housekeeper, but this place looked as if it had been ransacked. As she tried to step around the mess on the floor, the hem of her dress caught on a pile of books dumped on the floor. One of the books tumbled off the top of the heap and thumped to the floor.

The sound of rummaging in the bedroom stopped. The flashlight beam blinked out.

In the blinding darkness, Jill felt on the wall for the light switch and flipped it on. Nothing happened. Had Trevor forgotten to pay his light bill or—

A figure came barreling out of the bedroom. Jill tried to get out of the way, hearing the movement rather than seeing the person in the dark. She felt an object strike her hard on the head. Her knees buckled.

As she dropped to the floor, she heard the retreating footfalls, then the sound of her car engine and the squeal of rubber tires on the wet pavement.

Dazed, she stumbled to her feet and moved to the open doorway. Her car was gone. So was the driver. She turned toward the bedroom and the scent of the woman's perfume that still hung in the air.

What had the woman been looking for? And had she found it?

Jill felt her way in the dark to the bedroom door, remembering the candle she'd bought Trevor as a housewarming present. She stumbled through the mess on the floor to the nightstand beside his bed and felt around for the candle. The light from an outside yard lamp shone through the thin bedroom curtains. She could make out something large and looming on the bed.

She found the candle and matches. Striking a match, she touched it to the wick. The light flickered, illuminating the small room.

An open suitcase lay on the bed, piled high with Trevor's clothing. The closet doors stood open, the hangers empty. The same with the dresser drawers.

Like the living room, the bedroom appeared to have been ransacked. Or Trevor had obviously packed in a hurry. His clothes in the suitcase were a jumble. It was obvious that the other Scarlet had been looking for something in the suitcase.

Holding the candle up for better illumination, Jill took a step toward the suitcase. Her shoe kicked a

balled-up sheet of paper on the floor at her feet. She
bent down and picked it up. Smoothing the paper,
she held it to the candlelight. It was an eviction notice. Trevor was four months behind in his rent?
How was that possible? Even if he'd put all his
money into the island development, his parents were
wealthy. She realized that if he hadn't paid his rent,
he probably hadn't paid his electricity bill, either.

Head aching, she looked into the suitcase, still
wondering what the woman had been searching for.
Jill picked up one of Trevor's shirts. An airline-
ticket folder fell to the bed.

She lifted it carefully, afraid of what she was going to find. Inside was Trevor's passport and a one-
way ticket on a flight out of Kalispell *tonight,* final
destination: Rio de Janeiro, Brazil.

Brazil? Trevor hadn't just been planning to run
out on his rent and his electricity bill. He'd been
running out on her, as well. When had he planned
to tell her? At the party? And what about the other
Scarlett?

Jill leafed through the folder until she found the
receipt from the travel agent. Her hand began to
tremble. Trevor had purchased *two* tickets on a
credit card. One for himself. The other for his *wife.*
The name on the other ticket was Rachel Forester.

The other Scarlett? Is that what she'd taken from
the suitcase—her ticket?

Jill leaned against the bed frame, feeling dizzy
and sick. Trevor had been planning to marry someone named Rachel *tonight* and run off with her to
Brazil? It was unbelievable. She thought she

couldn't despise him more than she already did. She was wrong.

As she started to put the ticket back into the suitcase, she noticed the credit-card number on the receipt for the tickets. "Trevor, you really are a lousy bastard." He'd used Jill's credit card to buy the tickets for himself and his secret new bride.

Reeling, Jill stumbled out of the condo. Her head throbbed, and when she touched the bump on her forehead, her fingers came away sticky with blood.

All she wanted to do was go home and forget this day had ever happened. Forget Trevor. Too bad she couldn't forget what had happened between them in the cottage—before the other Scarlett had shown up.

As she drove downtown to her apartment over the bakery she owned, she told herself this night couldn't get any worse. But as she passed the bakery, she saw the sheriff's deputy car parked across the street. Two deputies got out as she parked the van out front rather than continue on around to the back entrance to the upstairs apartment.

She stood paralyzed with worry on the sidewalk as they approached, afraid it had something to do with her father. Gary Lawson hadn't been well enough to attend the party tonight. He'd said it was only the flu—

"Jill Lawson?" the taller of the deputies asked, the one whose name tag read James Samuelson. "Sorry to bother you so late. May we come in and have a word with you?"

She nodded dumbly and swallowed, her throat

constricting, as she shakily unlocked the door to the bakery and let them in.

"We're here about Trevor Forester," the shorter, stouter of the two said. He introduced himself as Rex Duncan. He took out a small notebook and pen.

She stared at the deputy. "Is Trevor in some kind of trouble?" Understatement of the year.

She could feel Samuelson studying her face. Past him, she caught her reflection in the front window. Her eyes were red and puffy from crying, and the bump on her forehead was now bruised and caked with blood around the small cut where she'd been hit.

"When was the last time you saw him?" Samuelson asked.

"Tonight. At the party." She saw the deputies exchange a look.

"Tonight? What time was that?" Duncan asked.

"About eight-fifteen."

"You're sure you saw him?" Samuelson said.

"I was with him until about…nine-thirty, then I left. Has something happened?"

The deputies exchanged another look.

"Please tell me what this is about," she said. "You're scaring me."

"Ms. Lawson, you couldn't have been with Trevor Forester tonight at the party," Samuelson said. "Mr. Forester was murdered during the time you say you were with him at another location. I think you'd better tell us why you'd make up such a story."

Chapter Two

As the woman stormed out of the lake cottage, Mackenzie Cooper pushed himself up from the floor on one elbow and groaned.

"Who the hell was that?" he asked the darkness, still stunned by what had happened between them.

Silently he cursed himself. When she'd come into the cottage while he was spying on the boat just off the shore, he'd kissed her, only planning to shut her up and keep her from giving him away. But one thing had led to another so quickly...

Damn. What had he been thinking? That was just it. He hadn't been thinking.

He felt dazed as he checked his watch. Nine-forty. He'd completely lost track of the time. Completely lost track of everything. Especially his senses.

He quickly dressed, changing enough of the costume so that he wouldn't be recognized as Rhett Butler. The last thing he wanted to do was run into either of the Scarlett O'Haras again tonight. In the mood they were in it could be dangerous. Another reason to hightail it out of here as fast as possible.

It was obvious the man he was supposed to meet

here had stood him up. Which, all things considered, was just as well.

But first, Mac had to know what the woman had thrown at him. Using the penlight he'd brought with him, he shone it around on the floor.

Something in the corner glittered in the light and he bent to pick it up. A diamond ring. The stone was a nice size, the setting obviously old. He pocketed the ring and started to leave, but spotted something else on the floor in the beam of the penlight.

It appeared to be a scrap of black fabric. He picked up the skimpy, sexy panties. Silk. Her scent filled his nostrils, momentarily paralyzing him with total recall of the woman he'd had in his arms tonight.

Suddenly he wished he could have seen her in these. But his tactile memory flashed on an image of her that was now branded on his mouth, his hands, his body and his brain.

It seemed the woman had thought he was Trevor Forester—her fiancé. At least he *had* been her fiancé until the other Scarlett O'Hara had shown up.

He swore again, realizing the magnitude of what he'd done. He'd just made love to the last woman on earth he should have!

Not wanting to leave any evidence, he pocketed the panties along with the ring, then moved to the cottage door to make sure the coast was clear. It was time to get out of here. He'd gotten more than he'd come for. And then some.

TREVOR DEAD? Murdered? Jill staggered, her legs suddenly unable to hold her.

Deputy Rex Duncan pulled out a chair for her at one of the small round serving tables at the front of her bakery and helped her into it. He then drew up seats across from her for him and Samuelson, who pulled a small tape recorder from his pocket, set it on the table, and clicked it on.

"There must be some mistake," she said, looking from one to the other of them.

"There is no mistake," Samuelson said. "That's why we're confused. Why would you say you were with Trevor Forester tonight at the party? Unless for some reason you think you need an alibi."

She stared at him, stunned. "An alibi? I was with Trevor in the lake cottage during the time I told you." She looked from Samuelson to Duncan.

Duncan shook his head.

She felt the blood leave her head. If she hadn't been in the cottage with Trevor... Oh, my God.

"Why don't you start at the beginning?" Duncan suggested as he handed her a napkin from the dispenser on the table. "You arrived at the party at what time?"

She took the napkin and wiped her eyes, panic making her hands shake. "About seven-thirty."

"Alone?" Duncan asked.

She nodded. "I thought Trevor would meet me at the party since he was running so late."

"Trevor Forester was your fiancé?" Deputy Samuelson asked.

She nodded, then glanced down at her ringless finger, the white mark on her lightly tanned skin where the diamond engagement ring had been. The deputies followed her gaze. She quickly covered her hand.

"I think you'd better tell us what happened tonight," Samuelson said. "It's obvious you've been crying. How did you get that bump on your head?"

She looked up at him, then at Deputy Duncan, and fought to swallow back the dam of tears that threatened to break loose. Trevor dead. Murdered. And the man in the cottage who'd been dressed like Rhett Butler...?

"The truth, Ms. Lawson. You weren't with Trevor Forester tonight at the party. So where were you?" Samuelson asked impatiently.

"I thought I *was* with Trevor," she cried, and saw them exchange another look. "I know this will sound crazy..."

"Believe me, we've heard it all," Duncan said, not unkindly. "Just tell us what happened."

She took a breath. "Trevor was supposed to pick me up for the party at six-thirty," she began. "We were going as Rhett Butler and Scarlett O'Hara." Jill told them how she'd gone alone to the Foresters at seven-thirty, waited for him in a room off the far wing until she'd seen the man she believed to be Trevor dressed as Rhett Butler duck into the lake cottage at eight-fifteen. She'd just looked at her watch—that was why she remembered the time. "It was just before the electricity went out."

Duncan nodded. "A transformer blew on that side of the lake about then. The man you saw, he had on a mask?"

She nodded and realized she'd only gotten a

glimpse as he'd gone into the cottage. Just an impression of Rhett Butler.

"So you went down to the cottage in a downpour to see him?" Samuelson asked. "Why not wait until the storm let up? Or he came up to the party?"

"I wanted to speak with Trevor alone first."

Samuelson raised an eyebrow. "About what? I see you aren't wearing your engagement ring."

"The truth is, I had planned to break off our engagement," she admitted, wondering if they'd already found her engagement ring in the cottage. She assumed they'd already talked with Heddy and Alistair. Had Heddy told the deputies how upset Jill had been? That she'd planned to break the engagement?

"Why break up?" Samuelson asked, eyeing her closely.

She shook her head, not knowing where to begin. "I had hardly seen Trevor lately, and I just felt that we shouldn't be getting married."

"You said *had* planned to break off your engagement. Did something change your mind?" Duncan asked.

"Actually, Trevor did—at first. Or at least the man I thought was Trevor." She could see the deputies' skepticism. She hurriedly told them how the electricity had gone out, how in the darkness the man she thought was Trevor had grabbed her, kissed her, seduced her—all without a word spoken between them.

She dropped her gaze to her hands, clasped in her lap, for a moment, the shame and humiliation almost getting the better of her as she thought of what she'd done with a stranger. She had opened herself up to him. At the time she'd thought it was the darkness that had let her put all her inhibitions aside and make love as she'd never made love before—completely.

When she looked up, she saw they didn't believe a word she'd said. "It's true! I can prove it. Someone saw us together. A woman." She groaned silently, mortified to have to tell them.

"What woman?" Duncan asked.

Jill looked at him and realized she didn't have a clue who the woman was. Reluctantly she explained how it seemed Trevor had planned to meet, not her, but the other Scarlett in the cottage. "The woman saw us, became angry and left."

"I thought it was dark inside the cottage?" Samuelson said.

"It was, but there was a flash of lightning as she opened the door," Jill said.

"You didn't see the man in this flash of lightning?" he asked incredulously.

She shook her head, remembering how he'd spooned her against him, the gentle way he'd nuzzled the nape of her neck, his breath on her bare, hot skin… "I was facing the door and he was… behind me."

"What did you do after this woman interrupted the two of you?" Duncan asked.

"I realized Trevor—" she heard her voice break "—I mean, the man I thought was Trevor…had just made love to the wrong woman. I hurriedly dressed, threw the engagement ring at him and left."

"You never saw his face?" Duncan asked.

She shook her head.

"You must have been furious," Samuelson said.

"I was hurt." She dropped her gaze, remembering the depth of that hurt because of what they had just shared.

"Did you tell anyone about this?" Duncan asked.

"No. I left by the side yard. I was upset. I certainly didn't want to talk about it." She saw the way they were both looking at her and added, "I think the woman's name might be Rachel, but you'll have to catch her tonight before she gets on a plane for Brazil."

Samuelson raised a brow. "Why would you think that?"

Jill told them about almost being run off the road by her own red Saturn and how she'd followed it, thinking at first that Trevor was driving the car, since he was the one who'd borrowed it the last time she saw him.

"The front door was open. Someone was in the bedroom, rummaging around, using a flashlight," she continued. She told them how the person had come flying out, hit her and left in her car. "I caught a whiff of the same perfume I had smelled when the woman opened the door to the cottage."

"So you think it was the same woman," Duncan said.

"Was she still wearing her costume?" Samuelson asked.

Now that Jill thought about it… "No. She must have had a change of clothing with her." Maybe her traveling wedding suit since, if she was Rachel, she and Trevor were headed for a justice of the peace and a plane, it seemed. "If you've been to his condo, you know that Trevor was running away to-night with a woman named Rachel." Their poker faces told her nothing.

"We'll try to find your car," Duncan offered. "And this woman." His tone implied, *If she exists.*

"Thank you."

Samuelson was shaking his head. "Come on, Ms. Lawson, how could you have made love with a man and not realized he wasn't your fiancé?"

Her face flamed with embarrassment. "Trevor and I had only been...intimate once." She thought of the differences, not just in the lovemaking but in the man's body. She'd believed it was because Trevor had been doing manual labor for the past few months. He was so much more muscular. Stronger. More...forceful. He'd lost some weight and was leaner—just like when she'd seen him recently. And he'd promised her that tonight would be different. Oh, and it had been, she thought, fiddling nervously with the silver charm bracelet at her wrist.

"Heddy Forester says when she saw you at about seven-forty-five, you were very upset with Trevor," Samuelson said. "She says she thought you left right after that. You have keys to the Foresters' boats, right?"

"Yes, but—"

"In a ski boat, it takes how long—ten, fifteen minutes?—to get down the lake to the island," he asked.

She stared at him. "Trevor was killed on the island?" What was he saying? That she would have had plenty of time to get to the island, kill Trevor and return to the party—and the cottage. "I told you—"

"Yes, you told us," Samuelson interrupted. "You were in the cottage. Then how do you explain the fact that Heddy Forester saw you get out of a boat at the dock just a little before nine-thirty?"

"It wasn't me. It must have been the woman I told you about, the one who was also dressed as Scarlett O'Hara."

It was clear Samuelson didn't believe her.

"Was there anything about her you can remember other than the costume?" Duncan asked.

"All I saw was her silhouette in the doorway. But I think I'd recognize her voice if I heard it again." A strident, high-pitched voice.

Duncan shifted in his chair. "When was the last time you were on Inspiration Island?"

"I've never been on the island. Trevor didn't want me seeing it until everything was finished. He said he didn't allow anyone but crews on the island during construction, not even investors, if he could help it." She realized how stupid she'd been. Trevor had probably used the island as a place to spend time with the other Scarlett. Not that Jill cared to go out there, given the island's history. Maybe that was why she'd never pushed the subject.

"Do you know anyone who might have wanted to harm Trevor Forester?" Duncan asked.

She shook her head. "I would have said Trevor

had no enemies. But I realized tonight that I didn't know Trevor at all.''

''I think that will be enough for now.'' Duncan turned off the tape recorder. Both deputies pushed to their feet. ''We'll check out your story, Ms. Lawson. You might want to have someone take a look at that cut on your forehead.''

''It's fine.'' She told herself there was no reason to worry about anything. The man she was with in the cottage would come forward once he heard about the murder. Also the other Scarlett. Once the deputies found her car...

''When you search the cottage, you'll find my engagement ring I threw at the man as I was leaving.'' She cringed as she remembered what else she'd left behind. ''You'll also find some black silk...underthings of mine that I didn't take the time to collect.'' She was mortified that her risqué panties and bra would now be...evidence in a murder investigation. Her face burned. ''All of which prove I'm telling the truth.''

Duncan looked sympathetic, but doubtful. ''They prove you were in the cottage. Not that you were with anyone. We'll get back to you. Please don't leave town.''

''I have no intention of going anywhere,'' she snapped. ''I have a bakery to run. I also have no reason to leave. I want to know who killed Trevor as much as you do. More so, since you seem to think I'm a suspect.''

''If you think of anything else, please give me a call.'' Deputy Duncan handed her his card.

She watched them both leave, feeling heartsick. The events of the night seemed surreal, a bad dream. Trevor murdered? Herself a suspect? A chill skittered over her skin. Was it possible that she'd found the passion she'd always longed for—in the arms of a total stranger?

MACKENZIE COOPER left the Foresters' and walked down the road in the pouring rain to his pickup. He'd had to park a half mile back up the lane because of all the cars. Those cars were gone now, and when he turned to look back, he saw something that sent his heart pounding. The sheriff's car was parked near the rear entrance of the house.

Getting into his Chevy truck, the camper on the back, he drove north down the narrow, winding lake road toward Bandit's Bay Marina, where he kept his houseboat. What had happened to cause the sheriff to go up to the house? He had a feeling he didn't want to know.

At the Beach Bar at the end of the pier at the marina, he ordered a beer. ''What's all the excitement?'' he asked the bartender.

''Trevor Forester was murdered tonight,'' the bartender said.

Mac felt as if he'd been kicked in the gut. Trevor was dead and Mac had just slept with his fiancée. Talk about bad karma.

He drank his beer, hardly tasting it, and listened to some of the locals talking about how Forester's boat was found floating about a half mile off Inspiration Island. A fisherman found Trevor lying in a pool of blood in the bottom of the boat. He'd been shot twice in the heart.

Murder was rare enough in this part of Montana. The last one was back in 1997 when some guy was killed on Hawk Island. What made this murder more tantalizing was that the victim was a local and that he was developing Inspiration Island, an island the men at the bar said should have been left alone. They hinted that the island was haunted, which was a good reason not to develop it.

Mac didn't buy into any of that mumbo jumbo. What interested him was that the locals hadn't liked Trevor. Partially because of the resentment they harbored for him and the Forester family money. Partially because Trevor was a jackass who also hadn't been paying his bills of late.

Mac sipped his beer, unable to shake the anxiety he'd felt the moment he'd seen the sheriff's car at the Foresters' lake house. It was just a matter of time before the sheriff found out about Trevor's call to Mac.

"I think someone's trying to kill me," Trevor had said on the phone yesterday, sounding scared. "I heard you're a private investigator. I need you to find out who it is before it's too late."

It had been Trevor's plan for them to meet at the party to discuss the job. Trevor had sent Mac a costume: Rhett Butler. They were to meet at the lake cottage at eight-fifteen tonight. Trevor would be arriving by boat.

Except Trevor never made it. Another boat pulled up. And Mac had recognized the man's voice as he came onto shore with a woman on his arm. Nathaniel Pierce. He and Mac had gone to university together. Mac had forgotten that Pierce had bought a place up this way.

He'd been watching Pierce from the window when the cottage door opened and the woman came in. The last thing Mac wanted to do was see Pierce, so Mac had kissed the woman to keep her quiet.

According to the discussion at the bar, Trevor's fiancée was a woman named Jill Lawson. While locals had little regard for Trevor, they had nothing but praise for Jill, although, like Mac, they couldn't understand what she saw in Trevor Forester. Jill owned a bakery in town called The Best Buns in Town.

A name that had more than a little truth to it, he thought. According to the locals at the bar, Jill was a hard worker, a fine-looking, intelligent young woman who baked the best cinnamon rolls in four states, not just in town.

If the locals knew about Trevor's other woman, they weren't talking. Mac listened to everyone speculate on who might have killed Trevor. It was clear no one had a clue. Mac finished his beer and walked down the dock to his boat, thinking of Jill Lawson. Worrying about her and wondering how she was going to take the murder of her fiancé, given what had happened tonight.

His houseboat was basically a box on pontoons, containing just the basics for living. He had it docked at the farthest slip at the end of an older section of the marina. The cheap seats.

The boat wasn't much, but it was home. It had a flat roof, with a railing around both the bottom and top decks, a retractable diving board and a slide that he'd used more for escape in the past than for swimming.

He entered the houseboat cabin without a key—he never bothered to keep the place locked—and was instantly aware that someone was inside waiting for him. He heard the telltale squeak of his favorite chair, but he'd also developed a sixth sense for unwelcome company. It had saved his life on more than one occasion.

Drawing his weapon from his ankle holster, he moved soundlessly through to the living area at the center of the cabin. He aimed the gun at the person sitting in the dark in his chair and turned on a light.

"I do like a cautious man," Nathaniel Pierce said as he looked up from the recliner where he was lounging, a bottle of Mac's beer in his hand.

"Pierce," Mac said.

The man was tanned, his body lean, his hair blond, his eyes blue, and even dressed down in jeans, a polo shirt and deck shoes, Nathaniel Pierce reeked of money. Old money.

Mac put the weapon away, walked to the small kitchen, pulled a bottle of beer from the fridge and twisted off the cap, pretty sure he was going to need a drink.

It wasn't every day he came home to find Nathaniel Pierce sitting in his living room in the dark waiting for him. Mac thanked his lucky stars for that. He and Pierce had been roommates at university—actually at several Ivy League universities, which they attended during a troubled period in both of their lives. They hadn't been friends for years.

Finding Pierce here made him nervous—and wary. "Slumming?" Mac asked.

Pierce laughed with only mild amusement.

"I'm sure you've heard that Trevor Forester was murdered tonight," Pierce said.

So much for small talk. "Trevor Forester?"

Pierce smiled. "I saw your truck at the party, but I never did see you."

Mac took a sip of his beer, wondering what Pierce was doing here. More importantly, what his interest in Forester was, or in himself, for that matter. "You hanging out with people like the Foresters?" Pierce had always been an old-money snob. Sure, the Foresters had money, but it was new and not nearly as much as the Pierces'. It was like the difference between a hot dog and beluga caviar.

"It's a small community," Pierce said in answer.

Not that small.

"I'm curious what you were doing there." Pierce took a swig of beer and smiled as if enjoying the taste. Not likely.

"I had an invitation." Mac put his feet up on the coffee table and downed half his beer, telling himself he was nothing like the man sitting in his recliner. True, they looked alike and were both thirty-six. At six-four, Pierce was a couple of inches taller, carried a little more weight and his hair was blonder, his eyes bluer.

And they came from the same backgrounds. Mac

had tried to overcome his. He'd chosen the worst possible career and lived on his houseboat on one lake or another or in the camper on the back of his truck. He kept a small office in Whitefish, Montana, where his sister lived, and he checked in every week or so, taking only the jobs that interested him.

He drank beer, dressed in old blue jeans, ragged T-shirts and Mexican sandals. Most days he was as close to happy as he could get, all things considered.

Clearly Pierce found all of that amusing, as if he thought Mac tried too hard to disguise who he was. A rich kid from old money. Just not as rich as Pierce.

Nathaniel Pierce loved being rich and flaunted it—when he wasn't slumming, like tonight. He believed it was the privileged's duty to acquire more wealth.

Mac, on the other hand, liked working for a living. He didn't require much. What he did require was a purpose in life. He thrived on challenging himself, both mentally and physically. That was why he'd gotten into private investigation.

"What is it you really want, Pierce?" he asked, deciding to cut to the chase.

"I told you, I want to know your interest in the Foresters. I wasn't aware you even knew them."

Mac smiled as he got to his feet. "It's late. I'm tired. I've had a big night."

Pierce didn't move. "I have a job for you, Mac."

"I already have a job."

His old friend lifted an eyebrow. "I'll pay you

double what you're getting from your current client.''

Mac smiled at that. His current client was dead. ''You know waving money at me is a waste of time.''

Pierce nodded, smiled and slowly pushed himself to his feet. ''I do know that about you, Mac.'' He said it as if he found that to be a flaw in Mac's character. ''Why don't you come out to my ranch, say in the morning about nine? I have a little place down the lake where I raise a few buffalo.''

Little. Right. Mac sighed impatiently. ''I told you—''

''You're already on another job. Yes, you told me.'' Pierce picked up a plain black videotape from beside the recliner. Mac hadn't noticed that Pierce had put it there. ''Take a look at this. If you still aren't interested...'' Pierce shrugged and tossed Mac the tape.

Mac caught it and watched Pierce leave. He stood there, listening to Pierce retreat down the old wooden dock until the footfalls became too faint to hear. Then he looked down with apprehension at the videotape in his hand.

What the hell was on this? Something that Nathaniel Pierce was confident would change Mac's mind about the job offer.

That alone was enough to make Mac nervous as hell. But to find Pierce sitting in the dark on the houseboat drinking beer, waiting...

Mac walked over to the VCR, turned on the TV, popped in the tape and hit Play. The images were blurred, everything a grainy black and white. The tape appeared to be a security surveillance video.

In the soundless recording were three people. Two wore ski masks, one of whom carried a sledgehammer. A third stood just out of the camera's view, but part of that person's shadow could be seen against the side wall.

Mac watched as the one with the sledgehammer worked to break through some expensive-looking wood. The other man in the ski mask had his back to the camera. The third appeared to be just watching, but the other two would glance back at him from time to time and say something Mac couldn't make out.

After a few minutes the hammer had made a large hole in what appeared to be a hidden compartment in the wall. The other masked man pushed the one with the sledgehammer out of the way and took a metal box from inside the compartment. The box looked to be about eight inches square and three or four inches deep. There didn't seem to be anything else in the hole in the wall because the men turned and left, disappearing from the camera's lens.

The videotape flickered, and the setting changed to outdoors. An old Ford van, dark in color, sat with the engine running, and the driver's face was captured on film. He was watching out the windshield, looking very young and very nervous. He was the only one not wearing a mask.

An instant later the two men in ski masks emerged from the house and ran toward the van. As they ran, they ripped off their masks. Mac's heart stopped.

One of the men was Mac's nineteen-year-old nephew Shane Ramsey, who was supposed to be in Whitefish with Mac's sister.

The other man running toward the getaway van was Trevor Forester.

Chapter Three

Mac couldn't sleep. He lay sprawled on his back in the bed, staring up at the ceiling, afraid to close his eyes. When he'd closed them, his thoughts closed in on him, an unsettling mix of pleasure and pain.

Even the pleasure was painful. He'd promised himself in his youth that he wasn't going to be one of those men who had regrets. Not like his father. Or his father before him. That was why he lived the life he did. On his own terms.

What a joke. He knew regret as keenly as he knew sorrow. And tonight would be a night he knew he would live to regret.

He gave up on sleep, got up, pulled on his jeans and, taking a cold beer from the fridge, wandered out on the deck to sit in the cool darkness.

The marina was dead quiet. The lake was calm under a limitless sky of dark blue velvet and glittering stars. He closed his eyes and tilted the mouth of the bottle to his lips. The glass was cool and wet, the beer icy cold as it ran down his throat.

He opened his eyes. It was the darkness, he realized. The blackness behind his eyelids that stole any chance of sleep. The same kind of blind darkness that would always remind him of the intimate inkiness inside the cottage—and her.

He smiled to himself wryly, remembering. He'd been lost the moment his lips touched hers. She'd stolen his breath, taken his pounding pulse hostage and carried him away to a place he'd sworn to never go again. Never find again even if he'd been tempted to look.

And what surprised him was that she'd seemed as blown away by the experience as he'd been. Something had happened tonight in the cottage, something that scared the hell out of him, because it made him feel as if he'd boarded a runaway freight train that couldn't be stopped. And now all he could do was wait for the inevitable train wreck.

He'd known that in one split second, one moment of weakness, life could irrevocably change. Mac had seen his father go from wealthy to piss poor in one of those seconds. The man's reputation ruined. His life destroyed. How many times had his father wanted to take back that instant in time?

Mac had always sworn he wouldn't end up like his father. He'd live his life, take on little baggage and never care too much about anything. He'd screwed up once and it had cost him more than he could bear. He wouldn't let it happen again.

He'd slipped up tonight in the cottage. He just hoped to hell he could weather the storm he feared was coming because of it. Every action had a consequence. The moment he'd kissed her. The moment he saw his nephew and Trevor Forester on that vid-

eotape. Both life-altering in ways he didn't even
want to think about.

And now he was working for Pierce. He swore.
Mac had few ways he could be coerced. His sister
and nephew were the only family he had.

Mac swore as he looked out over the dark lake
and thought about his nephew, a spoiled kid who'd
hated his grandfather for losing the family fortune.
Thanks to previous Cooper generations, though,
both Mac and his sister had substantial trust funds.
Just enough, it seemed, to make Shane crave real
wealth. Apparently the kind Nathaniel Pierce had.

Mac took another long drink of his beer, dreading
what Pierce would tell him in the morning. There
was a reason Pierce hadn't called the sheriff when
he'd been robbed. Mac knew Pierce hadn't done it
out of some loyalty to either Mac or his nephew.
Not Pierce. No, Pierce didn't want the cops knowing
about the metal box. Now why was that?

Not that it mattered. There was no way Mac
couldn't take the job. Not if he hoped to save his
nephew—although it might already be too late for
that. Someone had murdered Trevor Forester tonight. What were the chances it wasn't connected to
the robbery?

Mac also suspected that Pierce wanted him in on
this for reasons of his own that had nothing to do
with Shane. Shane was just a means to an end. And
that made Mac worry he was already in over his
head.

Leaning back, he stared up at the stars and knew
this restlessness he felt had little to do with Pierce

or Shane. As a breeze washed over the bare skin of his chest, he found himself drowning in memories of the woman from the cottage. He breathed in the night, the cool, damp scent of the lake. Closing his eyes, he was engulfed by the darkness and the feel of her. Jill Lawson.

Seeing her was out of the question. But he could no more forget her than he could the image of his nephew and Trevor Forester in ski masks on a grainy black-and-white videotape.

Pleasure and pain. He opened his eyes. A moment of weakness, he thought with a curse as he went inside the houseboat for his shirt, shoes and weapon. There was no turning back now.

AFTER THE DEPUTIES left, Jill locked up the front door and walked through the bakery to the rear of the building and the inside stairs that led up to the apartment.

With her father's encouragement and some money her grandmother had left her, she'd bought the two-story brick building right out of college and started her bakery, The Best Buns in Town. Gram Lawson was the one who got Jill hooked on baking in the first place. Grandpa had always said Gram made the best cinnamon buns in town.

From the time Jill was a child, she remembered Gram's house smelling of flour and yeast. She loved that smell. Especially tonight as she walked past the now-silent equipment, the sparkling kitchen. The mere sight grounded her and gave her strength.

As she started up the narrow back stairs, she felt

a draft and looked up. Her breath caught. The door to her apartment was standing open. She always kept that door closed and locked when she was gone.

She froze, heart pounding, and strained to listen. She heard nothing but silence overhead. Maybe she'd left the door open earlier. She'd been so upset about Trevor not picking her up on time...

Slowly, she climbed the stairs, all the horror of the night making her jumpy. Her head still ached from where she'd been hit and she felt sick to her stomach when she thought about Trevor. He'd been her first. The only man she'd ever been intimate with—until tonight. Dead. Murdered.

At the top of the stairs she stopped and listened again. Silence. Cautiously, she reached through the open doorway and flicked on the light, illuminating the small kitchen and breakfast nook. Beyond it to the left was the living room.

She blinked in disbelief and horror, a small cry of alarm escaping her lips. Her apartment had been ransacked—just as Trevor's had.

She heard a floorboard groan in the direction of the pantry. She started to turn, and then she saw him. A man wearing a black ski mask. She screamed as he grabbed her, but the sound was cut off by his gloved hand clamping over her mouth.

He slammed her against the wall, knocking her breath from her lungs, and struggled to pull a wadded-up rag from his pocket. She fought him, but he was too strong for her.

"Where is it?" he demanded, removing his hand from her mouth.

She tried to scream, but he quickly stuffed the nasty-tasting rag in her mouth, pinned her hands to her sides and flattened her body against the wall with his own. She couldn't breathe! Couldn't scream! He was going to kill her. Or worse.

"Where is it, bitch?" the hoarse voice demanded. "Where's the damned ring?"

The ring? She felt him pull hard on the silver charm bracelet at her wrist, felt pain tear down her arm. She struggled to get one leg free of his body and brought it up hard into his groin.

He let out a howl of pain, then reared back and hit her in the side of the face. As she slid to the floor, she heard him stumbling down the stairs and out of the building.

"As far as you can tell nothing seems to be missing?" Deputy Rex Duncan inquired. Duncan had done a thorough search of the apartment while Samuelson had gone down to the bakery to make sure no one was in the building.

Jill felt numb as she shook her head. She sat in one of her overstuffed chairs watching the deputy as he looked around the room. The paramedics had left, after telling her how lucky she was. She just had a cut on her forehead, a small abrasion on her cheek where she'd been hit and a scrape on her wrist. Neither blow tonight had been life-threatening. Nor was anything broken. No concussion. Just a headache from the first blow and a bruise to go with the other one.

"No signs of forced entry," Samuelson said as

he came up the steps and joined them in the living room.

Jill saw the two exchange a look. "What does that mean?"

"Is it possible you forgot to lock a door?" Duncan asked.

"No. They were all locked when I left for the party."

Samuelson was eyeing her again as if she was lying. "Unless you left the door open or the guy had a key."

"Who has a key to your apartment?" Duncan asked.

"My father and...Trevor had one."

"There were no keys on him other than the boat key when he was found," Duncan said.

Her blood went cold. "You mean the person who was in my apartment had Trevor's key?"

"We don't know that," Samuelson said.

Jill shook her head. "Trevor's key to my apartment was on the same ring as the one to my car. It stands to reason that whoever has my car has a key to this apartment."

"But you said you thought the person at the condo earlier who'd been driving your car was a woman," Samuelson pointed out.

She nodded, her head aching. "I smelled the perfume, but I never saw her. I can't be sure."

"You're sure the person in your apartment tonight was a man, though?" Duncan asked.

"Yes."

"Well, you said nothing seems to be missing."

Duncan glanced around. "The place has been tossed pretty good."

"He must have been up here waiting for you while we were downstairs in the bakery," Samuelson said. "It seems like we would have heard him." He turned to Duncan. "Make some noise," he said, and went downstairs again.

Duncan walked around, opened and closed drawers, moved furniture. Jill watched him, knowing what Samuelson was trying to prove. That maybe she herself had torn up this place, hit herself in the head, pretended she was attacked. And for what possible reason? To somehow cover up killing Trevor? She groaned and closed her eyes as she heard Samuelson come back up the stairs.

"Well?" Duncan asked.

"I didn't hear anything," the other deputy said, sounding disappointed. "The apartment is over the kitchen, not the coffee shop, and the building must be pretty well insulated."

"It appears he was looking for something in particular," Duncan said. "He didn't take the stereo or the TV or that expensive camera sitting right there on his way out. It has the same MO as the others."

The Bigfork area had been hit by dozens of burglaries over the past year, all believed to have been executed by someone local who knew exactly what he was after because of the items he didn't take.

With a start, Jill opened her eyes. "He asked me where my ring was."

"Your ring?" Duncan asked.

"I assume he meant my engagement ring since

it's the only one I wear—wore.'' She frowned and looked down at her bare wrist. "He broke off my bracelet." Her skin was raw where the chain had scraped her.

"What kind of bracelet was it?" Samuelson asked.

"A silver charm bracelet with a small silver heart with my name engraved on it," she said. "It was a present from Trevor." She could feel Samuelson staring at her again, wondering no doubt why the thief would take something like a cheap charm bracelet and not her camera.

"Is there someone you could stay with the rest of the night?" Duncan asked.

Her eyes felt as if they had sand in them. She was bone tired. Her head pounded. And she was sore and scared and angry and as vulnerable as she'd ever been. She just wanted the deputies to leave.

She wasn't waking up her father at this time of the night. Not when he'd been too sick earlier to attend the party. Nor was she going to a friend's. She just wanted to go to sleep in her own bed and pretend none of this had happened.

"I'm staying here. I'll lock the doors from the inside with the slide bolt. The windows are locked. I doubt he'll come back tonight, anyway." She saw the deputies exchange a look, but she didn't give a fig what they thought at this point.

"I suggest you get your locks changed," Duncan said. "In the meantime we'll see if Trevor's keys turn up. You have my number."

She nodded and followed them downstairs to lock

and bolt the door, then she checked the entry to the
bakery. Double locked and bolted.

Back upstairs, she headed for her bedroom. She
would straighten up the mess in the morning. Tonight all she wanted was to get out of this ridiculous
costume, take a hot shower and go to bed.

By the time she finished, she was so exhausted
she crawled between the clean sheets and fell into a
comalike sleep haunted by men with ski masks—
one masked man in particular.

JILL AWOKE to pounding. Without opening her eyes,
she reached for the man next to her in the bed, the
memory of their lovemaking so fresh—

Her eyes flew open, and her hand jerked back
from the empty space next to her, the memories
coming in nauseating waves. Trevor. Murdered.
Trevor, the man who had betrayed her.

She sat up, remembering the other Scarlet silhouetted in the doorway, the woman's words echoing
in her head. A woman who called Trevor ''darling''
and had planned to run away with him last night.

Jill groaned as she recalled that last night she, the
woman who'd made love only once before, and that
with her fiancé, had made love—an amazing and
passionate and wonderful experience—with a complete stranger. And now she was a suspect in Trev-
or's murder.

She wanted to bury her head under the covers and
stay there, but the pounding wouldn't stop and she
realized someone was downstairs banging at the outside door. She glanced at the clock, shocked to find

she'd overslept. It was almost three-thirty in the morning.

Hurriedly, she pulled on a pair of jeans, a sweater and her slippers. As she opened her bedroom door, she saw her ransacked apartment and remembered the man in the ski mask. A shiver of fear skittered up her spine.

In the wall mirror she caught a glimpse of herself. She looked as if she'd gone ten rounds in a boxing ring—and lost.

At the bottom of the stairs she turned on the outside light and was relieved to see Zoe Grosfield, her baking assistant. Zoe mimed that she'd forgotten her key, then mimed a heartfelt apology.

Oh, why hadn't Jill thought to call Zoe to tell her not to come in today?

"Hey," Zoe said as Jill unlocked and opened the door. "Sorry. You know me, airhead extraordinaire." She pretended to refill her head with air as she breezed in, bringing the fresh, cold morning with her.

Just the sight of Zoe cheered Jill immensely, and she realized that she needed to bake today, needed that normalcy and the comfort her work afforded her. She could lose herself in baking, and today that was exactly what she needed.

"So you want me to start the breads?" Zoe asked with her usual exuberance as she headed for the kitchen.

Zoe's hair was green today, spiked with a stiff gel that made her head look like an unkempt lawn. She'd filled her many piercings with silver and wore makeup that gave her a straight-from-the-grave look. Frightening. Especially at this hour of the morning.

Jill had thought twice about hiring Zoe. For one thing, she was young—only seventeen, not even out of high school. Cute as a pixie, but her makeup was heinous, her many piercings painful-looking and her neon-bright, short spiked hair changed color with frightening regularity. Jill had been afraid the girl would scare the older customers.

Plus, Zoe had an ever-changing string of boyfriends whose appearance rivaled her own. And it was no secret that the girl loved to party. Almost every T-shirt Zoe owned proclaimed it. Everything about Zoe screamed "unreliable bakery assistant."

But from the first day, Zoe had seemed fascinated by the workings of the bakery, so Jill had weakened and given her the job.

Zoe had proved to be a good worker, prompt and dependable. And Jill had felt guilty for judging the girl by her appearance.

Also of late, Zoe had fallen in love. Which wasn't rare. But this one had lasted for more than a week. Which *was*.

"Breads. That would be great," Jill said. "If you want to get started, I'll be right down."

"Rough night?" Zoe asked, eyeing her.

Had she heard about Trevor's murder? Jill knew from her glance in the mirror that she looked bad.

"Just a late night," she said. "That stupid costume I was wearing." She raised her hand to the knot on her head. It was tender. So was the spot beneath her left eye. "I kept running into things." So true.

Zoe nodded knowingly. "One of those hoop-skirt things, right? Man, can you imagine dressing like that all the time? Too weird. And in your case, too dangerous!"

Jill laughed. Yes, Zoe was exactly what she needed.

"I'll get some coffee going first," Zoe said. "You look like you could use a cup."

"Thanks, I really could." She was grateful that she wouldn't have to discuss last night—or Trevor. If Zoe knew about Trevor's murder she'd be asking a dozen questions. "I'll be down in just a few minutes to get going on the cinnamon buns."

"Cool," Zoe said, and headed for the bakery's kitchen. Beyond it, Jill could see the dark shapes of the tables and chairs of the small coffee shop. And beyond that the dark street. What caught her eye was a car parked across the intersection. A shiny black sports car. Was there someone sitting in it behind the tinted windows? Someone watching the bakery?

"Jill? Are you sure you're all right?"

She blinked and focused on Zoe, who'd turned to look back at her in concern.

Jill nodded. "Just tired." She hurried back upstairs to her apartment, ran a brush through her long brown hair and plaited it into one long braid down her back. After she brushed her teeth, she put on makeup, something she seldom wore, to cover the worst of the scrapes and bruises. Not great, but definitely better.

She tidied the apartment a little and returned to the kitchen to find Zoe hard at work getting the bread doughs started.

"How was *your* night?" she asked the girl, who was sifting flour into a large metal bowl. It was the way they started their days. With Zoe's stories about her dates, her parents, her friends and the latest love of her life, a guy known only as Spider. "Did you see Spider?"

"Finally." Zoe measured flour into the large floor mixer and sighed. "He promised to take me to a party, but he didn't show up in time."

Jill knew the feeling. "I'm sorry."

"He came around later, said he'd been working."

Working. Jill had heard that one before, too.

"But we went out on the beach, parked and talked." Zoe shrugged shyly. "He's the coolest guy I know. Older, you know. And he likes me." She grinned. "A lot. But I'm taking it slow. You know, kinda playing hard to get."

"Good idea," Jill agreed, curious about this Spider. Older. That was the first time Zoe had revealed that. "How much older?"

Zoe shrugged. "He drives a great car."

"Really?" Jill glanced out the front window thinking it might be a black sports car. But the car was gone.

"It doesn't happen to be black, something sleek and sporty, does it?" Jill asked.

Zoe laughed. "Not likely. It's old. You know, one of those cars from, like, the sixties that's been made cool again."

''Cool.'' Jill felt relieved Spider's cool car wasn't a black sports car. She knew she was just being paranoid, but then, she had a right to be, all things considered. She lost herself in making the cinnamon-roll dough.

It was hard not to worry about Zoe. The girl was too trusting, especially in light of the disappearances there'd been in the area over the years. Most were girls about Zoe's age who'd come to the lake for summer jobs. As far as Jill knew, none of them had ever been found.

Jill felt sick remembering the year she was sixteen and the close call she'd had. It had been the only time she'd hitchhiked. Her first and last time.

Carefully, she dumped the flour and yeast into the large mixer and turned it on low as she added the warm water. Work was exactly what she needed. Work that she'd loved since those early days in her grandmother's kitchen. Jill had always turned to work to help her get through the rough times, like four years ago when her mother died, or like the past few weeks when she'd known something was wrong between her and Trevor. This morning was no different.

What annoyed her was how naive she'd been. Why hadn't she suspected it was another woman? It seemed so obvious in retrospect. Was it possible there'd been more than one?

She assumed the other Scarlett and Rachel were the same woman. Unless Trevor had three women he was taking for fools. *That* could definitely get a man killed.

What amazed her was that whoever the other Scarlett had been, it appeared she'd planned to take Jill's place at the party—after Trevor broke his engagement. The sheer nerve of the woman! And the cowardice of Trevor! The only reason he'd have broken their engagement at the party was that Jill wouldn't have made a scene with other people around. What a jerk he'd been.

Jill tried to concentrate on the baking, but as hard as she tried, she couldn't stop thinking about last night and the man she'd made love with.

Each breath she took seemed to remind her of his kisses, each movement reminded her of his body, each sound reminded her of his soft groans as his hands and mouth explored her.

She felt herself blushing, followed by a drowning wave of guilt. Her fiancé had just been murdered. What was wrong with her? But her feelings toward Trevor had never been as strong as those she'd had toward a total stranger last night in the cottage. And to think that she'd "saved herself" for Trevor!

Why *had* Trevor asked her to marry him? And why had she accepted? They'd hardly spoken throughout high school. Even after college when she'd first opened the bakery, she seldom saw him. They ran in different social circles.

Then one day out of the blue, he'd asked her to a party at his parents' house. She'd been flattered. And over the next couple of weeks, he'd romanced her, pulling out all the stops with flowers, dinners at fancy restaurants, cards, phone calls and gifts, like the charm bracelet.

It had been the first gift he'd given her. But looking back, Jill had never felt as if his heart was in it. Even the one time they'd made love...

All the signs had been there. She'd ignored them. Because she'd wanted to.

But no matter her feelings for Trevor, her heart went out to his parents. Heddy and Alistair must be devastated. Their only child. Their precious son.

Had they even an inkling that Trevor was planning to run off last night? One-way tickets to Brazil didn't make it look as if Trevor and his new wife had any plans of coming back. Heddy must be crushed.

It just didn't make any sense, though. Trevor had had such plans for the island development. In fact, she remembered that when Alistair had the chance to buy the island, Trevor had practically begged his father to give it to him.

''Someone else will develop it otherwise,'' Trevor had said. He'd been in a frenzy the day Alistair was to sign the papers, afraid something might go wrong and the island might end up in someone else's hands.

What had happened out on the island the past two months? She'd heard rumors that there had been problems. Setbacks, delays, accidents on the island, which of course only added to the stories of the island's being cursed, haunted. When she'd asked Trevor, he'd said someone had been sabotaging some of the equipment. Kids.

She shook her head, shocked that the deputies thought she might have had something to do with

Trevor's death. With a start, she reminded herself that she needed an alibi, as crazy as that was. If either her mystery lover or the other Scarlett didn't come forward soon, she'd have to find them.

Trevor's girlfriend might be easier to locate, Jill realized. At least, Jill thought she'd be able to recognize the woman's voice if she ever heard it again.

Recognizing the mystery lover was a whole different story. She wouldn't know him with his clothes on! Not even naked unless it was by touch. Her memory of him was all tactile, sensual, physical. He'd smelled like the storm. No aftershave or cologne. His body had resembled Trevor's enough to fool her. Only more muscular, more solid.

She fanned herself at the memory and suddenly had a horrible thought. Why had the man been dressed as Rhett Butler? Had he known what Trevor would be wearing last night? Had he purposely tried to take Trevor's place? Or—

The large empty bun pan slipped from her fingers and crashed to the floor. Oh, my God. Was it possible she'd made love with the killer?

Chapter Four

Nathaniel Pierce smiled as he opened his front door to Mac just before nine the next morning.

"Mac," Pierce said cheerfully, and motioned him inside the massive ranch house, which was set back in the pines on the mountainside overlooking the lake. The interior decor was a combination of antlers and leather, rock and wood, antiques and Americana.

Pierce led the way through the huge living room, past a wall-size black-and-white photograph of a pasture running as far as the eye could see. In the foreground stood a massive herd of buffalo.

"Buffalo—it's the new beef," Pierce said when he saw Mac looking at the mural. "That was taken on part of my ranch," he said proudly. "Come out to the sunroom."

Mac followed him through the house to the screened-in room. Snowcapped peaks poked up from the horizon. In between was the blue-green of the lake. Mac took a look through the high-powered telescope aimed at the north end of the lake. He wasn't surprised to see that it was sited on the marina where his houseboat was docked.

He swung the telescope slowly southward, down the wooded lakefront. The view of the Foresters' home on the water, including the cottage, was damned good. A little farther south, Inspiration Island. Even the bay where Trevor Forester's boat and body had been found could be seen from here through the high-powered lens.

Was it possible Pierce had witnessed the murder?

"So what do you think?" Pierce asked.

Mac wasn't sure if they were talking about the ranch or the view, the burglary or the videotape, or the telescope and what could be seen through it from here.

"Amazing," Mac said, pretty much covering it all as he stepped away from the telescope to stand at the window.

Pierce smiled. "Quite the view, huh?"

The view was incredible. From here, the lake gleamed like a crystal ball. Mac stared at the water, afraid he could see the future in all the blue. "That was an interesting videotape you gave me. I'm surprised the sheriff hasn't already nailed the men responsible."

Pierce laughed. "You know I didn't call the authorities. Juice or coffee?"

Yes, Mac knew. He turned to find Pierce standing next to a table, holding a pottery pitcher in his hand, waiting expectantly.

"I had this juice flown in from Hawaii," he said.

"There's nothing like fresh pineapple juice, don't you think?"

"Yes, it's amazing what money can buy," Mac said. "Or there's always blackmail. And what can't be bought or blackmailed can always be stolen, right?"

Pierce smiled. "You have such a wonderful grasp of life's finer points."

"It must be annoying, though, to have your already stolen property be stolen," Mac said. "In fact, it must really piss you off. I'll bet that's why you don't seem at all broken up over Trevor Forester's death."

"Trevor was a...thief."

Among other things, Mac thought. "Isn't calling him a thief a little like the pot calling the kettle black?"

"There's a difference between someone who steals for money or revenge and someone who appropriates because they appreciate the value of what they're stealing."

"Right. So which was it?"

"I beg your pardon?" Pierce said.

"Was it money or revenge that Trevor Forester stole for?"

"Who knows and why does it matter?" Pierce filled both glasses on the table with juice. "You must try this."

"It matters," Mac said taking the glass Pierce offered him, "especially if you killed him."

His former classmate feigned shock. "You think I could kill someone?"

"No," Mac said, glancing at the telescope. "But you would hire someone to."

Pierce smiled. "I'm trying to hire *you* and I know you don't kill people—except in the line of duty. Now why would I bother to hire you if I'd already taken care of the problem?" He shook his head. "I just want my property back. If the men were all to die before I got it, now, that would be unfortunate." He waved a manicured hand through the air. "What do you think of the juice?"

Mac downed the pineapple juice and licked his lips. "Delicious. What was in the metal box?"

Pierce took a small sip of his own juice, obviously not wanting to be rushed. Either that, or he was hesitant to tell him. But then, Pierce had little choice if he hoped to get the contents back. "Some rather rare coins."

"How rare?"

Pierce lifted a brow. "Rare enough that I'm going to the trouble of hiring you to get them back."

Mac cocked an eyebrow. "That rare."

"They're priceless, all right? They're a set of Double Eagle twenty-dollar gold pieces. There is a Liberty figure on the front and an eagle on the back. Since I know you don't collect coins, why be more specific than that?"

Mac didn't know anything about rare coins, but he had seen an article in the paper the previous year about the world's rarest coin. A 1933 Double Eagle that fetched $7.59 million at auction. Back in 1933 President Roosevelt had decided to take the nation off the gold standard, so he'd ordered that all the newly minted twenty-dollar gold pieces be melted down. Someone had illegally smuggled the coin out, and it had ended up in the collection of Egypt's King Farouk. The coin disappeared again and finally turned up when a British coin dealer had tried to sell it to an undercover secret service agent.

Mac wondered what the history of Pierce's coin set was and was glad he didn't know. "How do you know the thieves haven't already fenced the coins?"

Pierce shook his head. "The burglary was two months ago. The coins would have turned up by now."

"Two months ago?" Mac couldn't have been more shocked. "And you're just now getting around to hiring me?"

"I'd hoped Trevor would try to sell the coins," Pierce said. "I have a few…contacts. The coins are worth much more as a set. I would have heard about it. The coins were the only thing Trevor took, so he knew what he was getting. He wouldn't have split up the set. You do realize that Trevor's the one who's been burglarizing all the houses in the area, don't you?"

"What makes you think that?" Mac had to ask.

Pierce gave him a pitying look. "It stands to reason. Trevor knew all the people who were robbed because he attended the same parties they did, he could never have enough money, and he thought he was above the law."

"You just described yourself," Mac noted.

Pierce laughed. "Yes, well, my grandfather and

Trevor's were…acquaintances, but my grandfather had more money.''

"I've always wondered," Mac said, "why your father sold the island to the Foresters."

"To make a profit," Pierce snapped, and turned his back to pour himself more juice.

"Really? I didn't know he needed the money."

"My father won the island years ago in a poker game," Pierce said.

"Really?" Mac hadn't known that. He'd just assumed the island had been part of the land that Pierce's grandfather had bought up around the lake years ago. But he could see why Pierce's father had wanted to unload it. Even if half the stories about the island were true…

"Yes, really. Anyway, the island's always had questionable value and the potential for lawsuits if anyone got hurt on it. Trevor seemed to think he could make money by turning it into an upscale resort. What a fool. Now the island is worth even less."

"How did Trevor know about the coins—or where in your house they were hidden?"

Pierce turned away from Mac and faced the view for a moment. Then he turned back. "I hate to admit this, but a stupid indiscretion on my part."

"A woman." Mac shook his head. "Showing her the ranch wasn't enough? You had to show her the coins? Did you tell her the house's security code, as well?"

Anger flickered in Pierce's gaze, but it was brief.

Pierce hid it with a smile. "I like to think it was the alcohol I'd drunk that night."

It didn't take a rocket scientist to figure this one out. "She had some connection to Trevor Forester."

"I guess so." Pierce shrugged. "As you would say, I was slumming."

"Who was she?" Mac asked, afraid of the answer. He didn't even want to consider that he and Pierce had more in common than money and the universities they'd attended.

"You really don't think I remember her name, do you? She was just some shapely brunette with long legs and amazingly large breasts. I think her name was Rainie or Rita, something like that."

Not Jill Lawson. One of Trevor's other women. Mac knew if he had any sense at all, he'd walk away from this. No, he'd run.

"You let her watch you deactivate the security system?" Mac asked in disbelief.

"I guess the woman was less of an airhead than I thought and a whole lot less drunk than she acted."

Pierce must have been very drunk. Also it wasn't like him just to let this woman get away with what she'd done without some sort of retribution. "What are you going to do about her?"

"All I want is the metal box and its contents back and to forget this ever happened. I'll just chalk it up to experience."

Why don't I believe that? Mac thought. "I'm going to need to know who the players are."

"They're all on the videotape," Pierce said.

Mac shook his head. "Not the one standing behind Trevor."

"What?"

"The shadow on the wall. Someone was standing behind Trevor, maybe giving the orders," Mac said. "Or maybe just along for the ride."

"I guess I didn't notice more than three people, counting the driver, in the video," Pierce said, still frowning. "Not that it matters. Like I said, I just want my…collection back. In fact, because of the history of the coins—"

"You mean because they're stolen."

"—I'd prefer that you simply locate the box and let me take it from there. That way you never have to actually have the coins in your possession. Does that make you a little more comfortable with this?"

Not really. "The coins are probably long gone by now."

"I'm sure once you locate your nephew, he'll prove to be a valuable resource in finding them."

Shane Ramsey's value was debatable right now. Mac looked toward the lake again, the mirror-slick water reflecting the wisps of clouds floating overhead.

Under other circumstances, he would have bailed out on this job in a heartbeat. He'd learned early on to avoid jobs that made him uneasy. Usually his uneasiness was for a damned good reason. A reason that could get a man killed—and it almost had happened on more than one occasion.

"Trevor's death will make it harder to find the coins," Mac said, turning back to Pierce.

"If I didn't know you better, I'd think you were trying to get more money out of me for your fee."

Mac studied the other man. "Everything about this one feels off somehow."

Pierce nodded, his blue eyes hard as ice chips. "Yes, Trevor getting himself killed after stealing my coins does make it a little…unpleasant." Pierce shook his head. "With a killer out there, you must be worried that the same thing could happen to your nephew. Especially if he has my coins."

"ARE YOU ALL RIGHT?" Zoe cried, picking up the pan Jill had dropped.

Jill felt her eyes well up with tears. Suddenly she couldn't quit shaking. The cinnamon rolls were in the oven and several kinds of additional buns and breads were about to go in when the cinnamon rolls came out. Hours had passed, and she was exhausted from trying to act like everything was fine and nothing had happened last night.

"I just remembered a phone call I need to make," she said. "Can you handle everything for a while?"

Zoe nodded, still looking concerned.

Jill dusted her hands on her apron and headed for the small office off the kitchen. She closed the door behind her and looked up the number for Guises and Disguises.

"Hello," she said, her heart in her throat. "I need to find out about the Rhett Butler costume I rented for Trevor Forester. I need to know when he picked it up yesterday. Are you the manager?"

"Yes, Tony Burns. Remember, we talked when

you came in to reserve the costumes," he said. "As a matter of fact, I was going to call you this morning."

"Really?"

"Mr. Forester didn't pick up his costume."

Had someone else picked it up for him? The other Scarlett?

"The costume you had me hold for Mr. Forester is still right here. I just wanted to let you know that I will have to charge the deposit to your card."

If Mr. Burns had been in the room, she would have kissed him. Trevor didn't pick up his costume! That meant the man she'd made love to hadn't been wearing *Trevor's* costume. She dropped into the chair next to the desk with relief.

Then she reminded herself that it didn't necessarily rule out the man being the killer. He'd arrived by boat about the time Trevor had been killed. The deputies could be off fifteen or twenty minutes in their estimation of the time of death. Nor did it explain why he was dressed in the same costume Trevor Forester was supposed to have been wearing.

"Mr. Burns, how many Rhett Butler costumes do you carry?" Guises and Disguises was the only costume rental shop around.

"Two." He sounded suspicious as if she was trying to get out of paying the deposit.

"Who rented the other Rhett Butler costume?" she asked, and held her breath.

"If you're thinking we gave Mr. Forester the wrong costume…"

She was hoping that wasn't the case. Otherwise,

she was back to the man she'd made love to wearing Trevor's costume—and that was the last place she wanted to be. "You would have a record of who rented it, right?" she said, praying that was true. Unless Trevor had picked up the wrong costume, Mr. Burns would have the name of her mystery lover.

"Let me check." He sighed and laid down the phone. She waited. He finally came back on the line, his voice sounding not quite as confident. "There might be a problem."

She held her breath.

"The other Rhett Butler and Scarlett O'Hara costumes were rented by Trevor Forester."

Jill slumped in the chair. "You're sure?"

"Yes. I'm sorry. I guess Mr. Forester picked up the wrong costume."

Not necessarily. He'd just planned to go with a different Scarlett. Whoever the woman was, she'd planned to meet Trevor at the party. Jill wondered whose idea that had been. Trevor's? Or the other Scarlett's?

Jill suspected the latter, given that Trevor tended to avoid conflict at all costs. Two Scarletts at his parents' anniversary party spelled conflict with a capital *C*. But the other Scarlett had probably planned to meet Trevor in the lake cottage *after* he'd broken his engagement.

Could she despise Trevor more? She didn't think so, but she was reserving final judgment until all the facts were in. She suspected she might have just uncovered the tip of the iceberg when it came to how rotten he'd been.

"Of course I won't charge you for the deposit, since there seems to have been some mistake," the manager said.

"No, the mistake was on my part," Jill assured him. "Please, I insist you charge me for the deposit." Why not? Trevor had charged two tickets to Brazil to her.

Mr. Burns sounded relieved. "You are most kind for being so understanding."

That was her. Understanding. Her hand was shaking as she hung up the phone. Her mystery lover had been dressed in the only other Rhett Butler costume. Trevor's costume. She felt sick.

After a moment she picked up the phone and called her best friend, Brenna Margaret Boyd. Her family owned the Bandit's Bay Marina, but Brenna had gone into journalism and worked for the *Lake Courier,* helping out at the marina in her spare time.

"Brenna, it's Jill."

"Jill! I just tried to call you, but the line was busy. I just heard. How are you?"

Over the past few months, Jill had shared her concerns about Trevor with her friend. At least, the problems she'd had *before* last night. "Still in shock. I need your help."

"Name it."

With Brenna everything said between them was off the record, and Brenna had the resources to find out most anything. "The deputies seem to think I killed Trevor."

"No! That's crazy."

"That's why I need to know everything you've got on the murder," Jill said. "Even the gossip."

"I'll call you back from the coffee shop up the block. Two minutes?"

"Thanks." Jill hung up and waited. The newspaper was rumor-mill central. Brenna would have heard a lot more than could be printed in the paper.

The phone rang not two minutes later.

"Okay, you want the basics?" Brenna asked. "This is what will be coming out in the newspaper this afternoon. Trevor's boat was found floating northwest of the island at 8:45 p.m. His body was lying on the floor of the boat. He'd been shot twice through the heart at close range, making the sheriff believe Trevor knew his killer."

Jill felt sick. "What was he wearing?"

"Work clothes. Jeans, T-shirt, work boots. He and the clothing were dirty."

"So they think he'd been working on the island?" Jill asked in surprise, given that Trevor had told her he didn't have to go to Inspiration Island yesterday.

"He'd been working somewhere," Brenna said. "But since it was a Saturday, there wasn't anyone else working on the island. So it's unclear where he'd been. Still, the proximity to the island makes them think that someone followed him when he left to get gas and killed him out on the water."

"They didn't find anything that would indicate he'd had his costume with him?" Jill asked.

"No costume."

Okay, he hadn't been wearing the costume. It

wasn't in the boat. The killer hadn't taken it off Trevor's body and dressed him in work clothing.

It stood to reason that Trevor would have left his costume back at the condo. Obviously he'd planned to take his boat back to the marina at the condo and shower and change before the party. Unless he'd chickened out and decided to skip the party, given that two Scarletts would be waiting for him.

"No weapon's been found," Brenna continued. "No sign of a struggle, either. They haven't released the caliber of gun used."

"What about time of death?" Jill asked.

"Trevor bought gas at Heaven's Gate Marina at the south end of the lake just a few minutes before eight. The deputies found a receipt in his pocket with the time on it. The dock boy didn't notice which way Trevor went, but the sheriff's speculating he went to the island for some reason, then might have been on his way to his parents' house when he was shot."

"They're sure he was killed in the boat—not on the island?"

"Yes. And the dock boy remembers Trevor seeming nervous, upset. He kept looking at his watch. Trevor told the boy to hurry because he had to meet someone and it was about to storm."

Jill thought about the boat she'd seen just offshore about eight-fifteen, only minutes before she saw the man wearing the Rhett Butler costume and thought it was Trevor. Did the man have time to kill Trevor and get to the party? But that didn't explain the costume or why the man was in the lake cottage.

"Are you sure you don't want to come stay with me for a while?" Brenna asked.

"Thanks, but I need to keep the bakery open. I need to work right now to keep my mind off everything." She filled Brenna in on all that had happened, including the mystery lover in the cottage.

"You have no idea who the man could have been?" Brenna cried.

"Not a clue. Except he was built kind of like Trevor," Jill said, realizing how lame that sounded. "I need to find him or the other Scarlett—who might be the Rachel that Trevor was planning to run off with."

"Well, if Trevor and Rachel really were going to get married before they flew to Brazil, then they would need blood tests and a marriage license. They would have filled out a marriage-license application. Give me the name of the travel agent. Maybe he set it up for Trevor."

"I hadn't thought of that," Jill said, and gave her friend the information.

"I'll see what I can find. If you need anything else, just let me know. I'll call when I hear something."

"Thanks." She'd barely hung up the phone when it rang again. "Hello?"

"It's Alistair, Jill." Trevor's father sounded desolate.

"I'm so sorry about Trevor," she said. "I was going to call you this morning, once it was a decent time. You must be in shock."

"Yes," he agreed. "The sheriff was here all

night. It's beyond comprehension. How are you, dear?''

"Just sick. Who would want to hurt Trevor?"

"I wish I knew," Alistair said, then fell silent for a moment. "Could you come out here later? I really need to talk to you."

"Of course." They agreed on two o'clock. She wondered what he wanted to talk to her about. No doubt her relationship with his son. "How is Heddy?"

"Not good." He hung up, unable to say much more.

Zoe was icing a huge tray of cinnamon rolls when Jill came out of the office. "Was that about me?" she asked, looking worried.

Her question took Jill by surprise. "Why would it be about you?"

Zoe shook her head. "You know me, always in trouble of some sort." She sounded almost scared.

"Not this time," Jill assured her as the back door banged open as it did every morning at this time and Jill turned to see her father. Since Jill's mother had passed away four years ago, Gary Lawson stopped by in the morning for a warm cinnamon roll, a cup of coffee and a chat.

Jill loved the early-morning chats with her father, but this morning when she saw his face, she knew he'd heard about Trevor's murder. Her father had wanted Jill to have the kind of marriage he'd had with her mother, and for a while, it had looked as though Trevor Forester would give her everything she could ever want.

"Hi, honey," her dad said.

Just looking at him, she felt the tears she'd fought so hard fill her eyes.

"I'm so sorry, Jill," her dad said, pulling her into his arms. "You must be devastated. I cannot believe it myself. Who would want to murder Trevor?"

They both turned at the shriek and crash behind them. Zoe stood with a rubber spatula in her hand, icing dripping from it onto the floor, an almost empty pan of cinnamon rolls on the floor where it had fallen.

Zoe's black-rimmed eyes were round as plates, and she looked even paler than usual. "Someone murdered Trevor?" she asked in a hoarse whisper. "Oh, God. I'm going to be sick." She dropped the spatula on the counter and ran out the back door.

Jill stared after her, surprised by her reaction. Zoe and Trevor had never been close. In fact, Trevor thought Jill irresponsible and stupid for hiring the girl and hadn't hidden his attitude from Zoe. The two had never said more than two words to each other.

"Is she all right?" Gary Lawson asked.

"I'd better go see if she—" Jill stopped at the sound of Zoe's VW Beetle roaring away. "Oh, no! She was supposed to make deliveries this morning."

"Don't worry, I'll make them for you," her father said. "Why don't you plan on closing early today?"

She hugged her dad. "You are the greatest. Are you sure you feel up to this?"

"No problem."

MAC STARED at Pierce. "I didn't just hear you threaten my nephew, did I?"

"No, I was just saying… Look, I came to you so you could protect Shane," Pierce said quickly. "I'm willing to bet that one of the thieves killed Trevor for the coins. If Shane has them—" he held up his hands "—the same thing could happen to him. As far as Shane stealing from me goes, I have no hard feelings against him."

"That's right, you just want the coins," Mac said. "Retribution would be the last thing on your mind."

"Not my style."

Right. Mac recalled a time in college when Pierce had beaten another student within an inch of his life—over some girl.

Mac turned to leave, a curse on his lips. Why did his nephew have to steal from Nathaniel Pierce, of all people? And how had Shane gotten involved in the first place? It made no sense. Shane lived in Whitefish with his mother. What the hell had he been doing down here? And how stupid was that, getting caught on videotape?

"I'll let you know when I find your coins," Mac said as he left. It was all he could do if he hoped to save Shane. But if his nephew had anything to do with Trevor Forester's death, nothing could save him. If Trevor had graduated from burglary to murder, he was on his own.

Mac didn't look back as he walked to his pickup. It was a newer Chevy with a camper, his home when a case took him away from the houseboat.

As he pulled onto the road, he wondered where

to start looking for Shane. Maybe Shane had taken off after the heist with his share of the loot. But Mac had a feeling the boy hadn't.

He took out his cell phone and speed-dialed his sister's number in Whitefish.

She answered on the first ring. "Shane?"

"No, Carrie, it's Mac." He groaned silently at the worry he heard in his older sister's voice. "What's wrong?"

"Nothing, I was just hoping it was Shane," she said, sounding close to tears.

"You haven't heard from him?"

"Not for over two months," she said. "He was talking about taking a trip with some friends, so maybe he just—"

"Some friends?" Mac interrupted. "What friends?"

"I'm not sure. I called Oz and Bongo and Skidder, those are the guys he usually hangs out with. No one has seen him, but Oz's girlfriend, Mountain Woman, said she saw him with some guy called Buffalo Boy."

Didn't any of Shane's friends have real names? "She have any idea what Buffalo Boy's real name is?"

"No one's ever heard him called anything but Buffalo Boy." She was crying now. "I'm worried sick about Shane. I just have this awful feeling." Awful feelings ran in the family.

Carrie had probably done as well as she could raising Shane alone after her husband drowned in Flathead Lake a dozen years ago when Shane was seven. So far most of Shane's scrapes with the law had been relatively minor: shoplifting, vandalism, driving under the influence and disorderly conduct.

Now, at nineteen, it seemed Shane had graduated to a higher level of criminal.

"I'll see what I can find out," Mac told his sister, keeping what he knew to himself for now.

"You're the best, little brother."

Yeah. He made a few calls on the way back to the marina, talked to some of Shane's former friends, guys his nephew had dumped when he'd moved on to less-desirable types.

A guy nicknamed Raker told Mac that all he knew about Buffalo Boy was that he'd worked on a big ranch that raised buffalo. "Never said what ranch," Raker said, anxious to get back to flipping his burgers. "But Buffalo Boy and Shane were talking about going down there and maybe working for the summer."

Mac had a pretty good idea whose ranch it was. He called Pierce and asked if Shane had been on the payroll and wasn't surprised that his old friend didn't have a clue.

"I have people who run the ranch," Pierce said.

"Ask those people and get back to me."

"I can't see that it matters—"

"It matters." Mac hung up, wondering how much.

As he drove through Bigfork, he noticed the sign on a two-story brick building: The Best Buns In Town.

It was foolish. Dangerous. His worst plan yet. But

he had to see the woman he'd made love with in the cottage last night. Trevor Forester's former fiancée.

Mac knew he was taking a hell of a chance. He told himself it was nothing more than curiosity. The truth was, she'd been haunting his thoughts ever since last night and that damned first kiss. Too much was at stake to have any woman on his mind—especially this one.

The bakery was busy, all but one table occupied as he pushed open the door. A little bell tinkled over his head, and he was immediately assaulted by the warm sweet buttery scent of cinnamon rolls—and the knock-him-to-his-knees sight of Jill Lawson.

Chapter Five

Jill looked up as the bell over the door jangled and she saw the man come in. She gave him only a quick glance. The place was hopping, just as it was every morning at this time. Zoe hadn't come back. Jill had tried to reach her at home, but there was no answer. She was worried. Worried about Zoe's reaction to Trevor's murder.

Now Jill wished she'd had the sense to close the shop, but she'd needed to bake this morning to try to keep her mind off what had happened. Not that it had done much good.

"Can I help you?" Jill asked as the man walked up to the counter. At first glance he looked like a lot of summer people—thirtysomething, tanned, blond, dressed in cutoffs, T-shirt and Mexican sandals.

That was why she was surprised by the tiny shock of awareness that made her skin tingle and her gaze dart up to his. His eyes were hidden behind sunglasses, the mirrored kind, so all she saw was her own reflection and the startled, flushed look on her face before he pushed them up and rested them on his head.

He was boy-next-door handsome, yes. But with an edge. And he was obviously fit, his shoulders broad, arms muscular and matted with blond hair, legs long, tan and strong-looking.

That still didn't explain her reaction. Or his.

A lock of blond hair hung over his forehead. He looked like a man who was comfortable with himself, with his surroundings. So why did he seem surprised by her reaction to him? Startled by it? He was probably used to women falling all over him.

"I'd really like one of those cinnamon rolls," he said. "They smell incredible." He smiled then, almost tentatively, as if afraid of her reaction.

She returned the smile, hoping he didn't notice just how flustered he made her. "Would you like coffee with that?"

He glanced toward the empty table by the window. "Please. I could use the caffeine. Black."

She rang up his order and took the money he'd set on the counter. "I'll bring it over to you if you'd like to grab that seat."

Her hand trembled as she scooped a cinnamon roll from the pan and slid it onto a plate for him. It was just nerves. A delayed reaction to Trevor's murder. To everything that had happened.

But she knew what had her shaken was her reaction to the man in the cottage last night. Surely she wasn't now reacting like that to *all* men, was she?

She added a fork to the plate, poured a mug of

coffee and headed to his table, aware he'd been watching her intently the whole time. Probably wondering what her problem was.

"Thanks," he said as she put the coffee down in front of him. "This is a great place you have here. I wish I'd known about it sooner." He was studying her, frowning a little as his gaze skimmed over her bruised cheek and forehead.

"Are you here for the summer?" she asked, trying to make her usual conversation as his long, tanned fingers curled around the mug to move it out of the way so she could put down the plate with the cinnamon roll on it.

His fingers brushed hers.

The shock wave arced from her fingers through her body. She jerked back, dropping the plate the last couple of inches. It rattled down on the tabletop.

"Oh, I'm so sorry," she said, feeling foolish for jumping the way she had. Her fingers still tingled where he'd touched them, and her heart was pounding.

"My fault. Static electricity," he said. "It's the dry heat."

She nodded, momentarily distracted by his mouth, a generous mouth, the lips almost…familiar. "Have we met before?" She couldn't believe she'd said that as she raised her gaze to his. "I'm sorry, that sounds like a line. I didn't mean—"

"It happens to me all the time," he said easily. "I guess I have a generic look."

Generic? No. Like Trevor? Yes. His body was about average height. Muscular. A lot like Trevor's had been the last time she'd seen him. Except this man was stronger-looking, harder—

The bell over the door jangled, and she swung around to see Deputies Duncan and Samuelson enter the bakery.

"I'm not usually…" Words failed her as she looked again at the man at the table.

"You're swamped," he said. He seemed to study her. "It looks like you have everything under control."

She smiled at that because it was so far off base. Without another word, she hurried to the counter, the air thick with the scent of warm, cinnamony baked buns.

She couldn't believe the way she'd embarrassed herself. She shot a glance at the man she'd just served. He was watching the deputies with interest. Again she felt an odd jolt of…something familiar.

"We'll take a couple cups of coffee, black, and—" Deputy Duncan looked at Samuelson, who shook his head "—just one of your cinnamon rolls." Duncan smiled.

But Jill knew they hadn't come here for her coffee or cinnamon rolls. She rang up their order and took the cash Duncan handed her.

"Keep the change," he said. "When you have a minute, we'd like to talk to you." He and Samuelson headed for a table that had just been vacated.

Jill heard the kitchen door swing open and wondered how her father had gotten back so soon from making deliveries.

But it was Zoe. "I'm sorry," the girl said quickly,

looking contrite. "I didn't mean to run out like that. It's just that…"

Yes, it was just what? Jill waited.

"…I've never known anyone who was murdered before." Zoe's eyes were wide with genuine fear.

"It's all right," Jill said, and reached for Zoe. The girl stepped into her hug and held on to Jill with a force that surprised her. She'd always thought that nothing could scare Zoe. "We're all upset. Can you help finish up here? I think we'll close early."

Zoe nodded wordlessly. "I can stay as long as you need me."

"Great. Bus the tables and then start on the kitchen."

Jill filled two mugs with black coffee and scooped a cinnamon roll onto a plate, added a fork and, taking a breath, walked toward the deputies. She didn't know how much more of this she could take. She felt as if she was losing her mind.

Coffee breaks over, the bakery started to clear out. Except for the man at the table by the window—and the deputies sitting in a back corner.

She glanced toward the window, still surprised by her reaction to him. Hadn't she known she wouldn't be the same after making love to that man last night in the cottage?

She returned her attention to the deputies as she neared their table. Why were they here? Maybe they'd brought some good news. She was tired of running scared, waiting for them to arrest her for Trevor's murder. She was tired of feeling helpless.

And if it was bad news? Well, then, she'd find

her mystery lover or the other Scarlett. Or both. And
if that wasn't possible, she'd have to find Trevor's
murderer. Whatever it took to prove her innocence.

She wondered if she should get a lawyer, then
vetoed the idea. She had nothing to hide. Not anymore. She'd bared her soul to the deputies after bar-
ing everything else last night to a total stranger.

She put the two black coffees on the table, then
the cinnamon roll, and sat down, aware of the only
other customer watching her. "You wanted to ask
me something?"

MAC FINALLY GOT his heart to settle back down. He
couldn't believe her reaction. Or his. Coming here
had been beyond stupid. It was almost as if she'd
known on some level who he was.

He took a bite of the cinnamon roll. It was amazing. So was Jill Lawson. He knew he should just
leave. He'd found out what he'd come for.

She was bruised, but all right. Better than all right.
He'd been worried last night when he'd parked on
a street by her apartment and seen lights on and the
sheriff's department cars parked right outside.

There was no doubt that she was under a hell of
a strain, but she seemed to be holding up all right.
He picked up a newspaper from one of the other
tables and pretended to read it as he picked up what
he could of the deputies' conversation with her. Just
as he'd suspected, her apartment had been broken
into the night before.

But he was shocked to hear that the burglar had
still been on the premises when she'd returned and

that she'd fought him off. That explained the bruises. He swore under his breath. The burglar must have been after Pierce's damned coins and thought Trevor had hidden them in Jill's apartment. Until the coins were found, Jill Lawson was in danger, just as he'd suspected last night. The reason he'd spent the night in his truck outside her apartment.

He glanced at her. She was adorable, no doubt about that. Slim but nicely rounded in all the right places, a body he knew intimately and a face that reminded him of angels, as corny as that was. She had dark-lashed, intelligent brown eyes that complemented her apparent strength of character.

He watched her, impressed. He'd already found out that she'd started the bakery right out of college and had made a real success of it. He could understand why. This cinnamon roll was like none he'd ever tasted. But she also had to be a damned good businesswoman.

The emotions she evoked in him, however, came from some deeper place. It wasn't just her looks or her success. This woman had touched him.

He closed his eyes, letting the bite of cinnamon roll melt in his mouth, shocked at the sensory effect it had on him. Just as Jill did. What was it about this woman? She had captivated him in the cottage last night with a single kiss, but her cinnamon rolls could bewitch a man in ways he hadn't even dreamed.

He opened his eyes with a silent curse. What was he going to do about Jill Lawson? This mess had him between a rock and a hard place. He couldn't very well tell Jill about the coins without jeopardizing his nephew, let alone taking the chance that the sheriff would find out that Pierce had stolen the coins to start with.

Damn, what *was* he going to do?

"Ms. LAWSON, we spoke with several of Trevor Forester's neighbors," Deputy Duncan said quietly. "They told us about an argument you and Mr. Forester had a week ago Sunday."

She stared at the deputy. "I didn't see Trevor a week ago Sunday."

"Ms. Lawson, the neighbors saw you leaving after the argument with Mr. Forester," Samuelson said.

She tried to contain her anger. "No, what they saw was a woman driving my red Saturn. Obviously Trevor's *other* fiancée. The same one he rented the Scarlett O'Hara costume for at Guises and Disguises."

"Yes, we know that Trevor rented a Rhett Butler and a Scarlett O'Hara costume—and so did you," Samuelson said. "Trevor didn't pick his up."

"But someone picked up the other set," she said.

"Yes. The clerk recalls you picking up the costumes and discussing who was going to pick up the other Rhett Butler," the deputy said.

She shook her head in disbelief. "I only picked up the one costume. The clerk is mistaken."

"That is possible," Duncan acknowledged. "She admits she was busy with all the costume rentals because of the Foresters' big party."

"We searched the cottage," Duncan continued. "There was no ring or anything else of yours that we could find. Nothing that would indicate you had a liaison there last night. The bedsheets and cover weren't even wrinkled."

"We never made it to the bed," she said, her voice falling. "Someone took my ring and my underwear. That should tell you something." But what? Had her mystery lover taken the items? Why would he do that except to cover up what had happened there? She felt heartsick and changed the subject. "What about my car?"

Duncan shook his head.

"When you find it, you'll find this other woman." Right now it was the only lead Jill had to the other Scarlett. That and the woman's voice.

"We have deputies looking for your car," Samuelson said. "If it's out there, we'll find it." He leaned toward her. "Come on, Ms. Lawson, stop wasting our time. You weren't in the lake cottage making love with some complete stranger last night. You went to the island to see Trevor, didn't you? What happened? You had a fight? You'd found out about this other woman."

Jill tried to keep her voice down. "If I had killed Trevor, do you think I would be stupid enough to say I was making love to a stranger in the lake cottage right after?"

"People tend to not think things through when they're under a lot of stress," Duncan said. He sighed. "The problem we're having here is that you seem to think you need an alibi, and quite frankly, you came up with one that only makes you look even guiltier.''

MAC TOOK THE LAST BITE of his cinnamon roll, mentally kicking himself for coming here. Out of the corner of his eye, he watched the discussion between Jill and the deputies heating up and caught enough of it to deduce that the deputies thought Jill murdered Trevor Forester.

It hadn't dawned on Mac that she might need an alibi. He swore under his breath. He was her only alibi? Great. The problem was, he couldn't tell the deputies the truth for several good reasons.

Which meant Jill Lawson was on her own with the authorities. At least for the time being. It also meant he had to stay out of her sight. He didn't think it would take much for her to realize he was the man from the cottage last night. Little more than another accidental touch could trigger it.

But Mac was more worried that if he spent any time around her, he wouldn't be able to help himself. He'd do something stupid like confess all. Or worse, kiss her again, and he feared where that would lead.

He stole a glance at her, jolted again by just the sight of her, let alone the memory of the two of them last night in the cottage. He felt like a schoolboy. What the hell was wrong with him?

Worse, he found himself wishing Trevor Forester was still alive so he could kick his sorry ass. For cheating on Jill. For ever being her fiancé in the first place. For putting her in this position—and Mac, as well.

He couldn't believe what a jackass Trevor Forester had been. This morning Mac had checked out the engagement ring Jill Lawson had thrown at him. He'd found faint initials on the inside of the band. They appeared to have been filed down, making him even more suspicious about where Trevor had gotten the ring. Mac remembered what Pierce had said about suspecting Trevor Forester was the burglar who'd been robbing area houses.

He suspected, like Pierce's coins, Trevor had stolen the ring.

Mac had sent a description of the ring to an old friend of his, Charley Johnson, at the Kalispell Police Department, to see if the ring came up on any stolen-property list. From what Mac had learned at the bar last night, Jill and Trevor hadn't been engaged long and there'd been no recent burglaries. If the ring was stolen, then it could mean that Trevor Forester had been a thief for some time.

Not that any of that helped Mac figure out what Trevor might have done with the stolen coins. If the burglary was more than two months ago, the coins could be anywhere.

What bothered Mac was that it appeared someone thought the coins were still in Bigfork. Why else had Jill's apartment been hit last night?

"Everyone knows you and Trevor weren't getting along," one of the deputies said, his voice carrying. "You said yourself you were going to break off the engagement."

Jill had planned to break her engagement to Trevor *before* she'd come to the cottage?

Mac tried not to take too much pleasure in that. He kept reminding himself that what happened last night could never happen again.

He watched her worry her lower lip with her teeth, making him unable not to recall her mouth on his. Jill Lawson was a dangerous woman. Smart, pretty, competent, sexy, independent—the kind of woman a man could fall in love with, the kind who made a man think about settling down, something Mac had no intention of ever doing. Not again. Jill Lawson was the ever-after kind, and Mac hated Trevor Forester for having somehow gotten this woman to love him.

"Can I get you more coffee?"

Mac looked up to see a girl with green hair holding a coffeepot.

"No, I have to get going, but thank you," he said, aware that the girl had seen him watching Jill and the deputies. "This is the best cinnamon roll I've ever eaten. Please give my compliments to the baker."

"You got it," the girl said.

Mac slipped a generous tip under his cup, feeling the girl's gaze on him. He couldn't come back here again. It was too dangerous.

But he hated like hell to leave the deputies badgering Jill. He hated like hell to leave her alone. He feared that the man who'd searched her apartment last night hadn't gotten what he'd been looking for.

That meant he'd be back, and that meant Mac would be spending his nights watching her apartment.

In the meantime he had to concentrate on finding the coins and Shane during the daylight hours. Once Pierce had the coins again, Jill would be safe. Then if Jill still needed that alibi… Mac told himself he wouldn't let her go to jail—if it came to that. Damn, but he hoped it wouldn't.

As he rose from his chair to leave, the bell over the door jangled. A thirtysomething, dark-haired man burst into the bakery and made a beeline for Jill Lawson.

"I heard you think Jill killed Trevor Forester," the man said loudly. He was about Mac's height and size, his tanned arms corded with muscle, his face lined with squint lines from the sun. A man who worked outdoors.

"Excuse me, but this is sheriff's department business," the larger of the deputies said, getting to his feet.

"Oh, yeah? Well, I'm here to tell you Jill couldn't have killed Trevor," the man said. "She was with me last night. In the lake cottage." The man looked at Jill and added, "Making love."

Chapter Six

Jill scrambled to her feet. She was shaking her head, staring at Arnie Evans, telling herself it wasn't possible. "Arnie, don't make things any worse by lying."

"Could we discuss this in private in your apartment?" Duncan suggested. "Mr. Evans, if you'd please hold down your voice until we can go upstairs."

Jill glanced up. The man who'd been sitting by the window was standing next to his table, staring at them as if in shock. She couldn't blame him, given what he'd just overheard. "Yes, my apartment." She glanced at Zoe, who also looked stunned.

"Take care of closing up?" Jill said.

Zoe nodded. "Should I call…someone?"

"I'll be fine." Not if Arnie had been her mystery lover.

Zoe nodded, big-eyed as they left for Jill's upstairs apartment.

Once upstairs Arnie sat in one of her overstuffed chairs, looking bashful and shy as he glanced

around. Duncan put the cushions back on the couch
and sat down. Samuelson leaned in the doorway to
the kitchen, watching them all.

Jill didn't want to sit. She wanted to pace. But
she made herself take the other chair, the one farthest from Arnie, as if that could somehow distance
her from his…story.

"Are you telling me that this isn't the man from
the cottage?" Duncan asked her.

Oh, God, I hope not. "It can't be."

"She didn't know it was me," Arnie said sheepishly. "She thought it was Trevor. Okay, maybe I
let her think that. When I came up with the idea to
dress in the same costume as Trevor, I thought it
would be fun. I didn't mean for it to hurt anyone."

Jill wanted to pull the floor over her head. Arnie
Evans. Since kindergarten, Arnie had been Trevor's
shadow and her tormentor. Whatever Trevor did,
Arnie tried, usually failing badly. When he hadn't
been emulating Trevor as a boy, he'd been throwing
worms at Jill or putting gum in her hair or pushing
her down in the playground.

Jill had learned to avoid Arnie.

As they grew older, Arnie had done poorly in
school, not gone to college, ended up in construction
and now had to work for a living with his hands—
all just the opposite of Trevor.

What had always amazed her was that Arnie and
Trevor had been such good friends. She suspected,
knowing what she now knew about her former fiancé, that the reason was because Trevor loved being idolized. Trevor used to say that every man

should have a friend like Arnie—and then he'd laugh.

While Arnie hadn't taunted or teased Jill as an adult, she'd felt that he was jealous of her relationship with Trevor. And when she was around the two of them, she had felt like a third wheel. She knew that Arnie would do anything for Trevor. Anything.

"He's lying," she said. *Oh, please, let him be lying.* She could never have been seduced by Arnie Evans. And yet, physically, he *could* have been the man. He was about Trevor's height, but then, so were a lot of men. He'd worked construction since he was young and he was strong, lean and solid, just like the man from the cottage.

Even Arnie's stupid explanation for why he was wearing the same costume as Trevor made sense, if you knew Arnie.

Why was Arnie doing this? "He *has* to be lying."

The deputies questioned him about the time, the storm, power outage, everything. Arnie, to her horror, seemed to have all the answers.

"What name did you rent the costume under?" Duncan asked.

Arnie shrugged. "Trevor rented it. I knew he had an extra Rhett Butler costume on his hands. That's how I came up with the idea."

"Arnie was Trevor's best friend!" Jill cried. "That's how he knew about the extra costume. I'm telling you, he's lying. How did he even know I needed an alibi? Don't you see? He must have heard all this from his cousin who works at city hall, right next to the sheriff's department."

Duncan looked at Jill as if she'd lost her mind. Here was a man ready to provide her with an alibi, and she was doing everything in her power to challenge it.

"Is there any way you can prove you were the man with Ms. Lawson in the cottage last night?" Duncan asked.

Arnie nodded and pulled the silk bra she'd been wearing last night from his pocket, dangling it before them.

Jill was going to be sick. And just when she thought things couldn't get any worse.

No WAY! Mac couldn't believe what he'd overhead just before the deputies went upstairs with Jill and the man she'd called Arnie. Arnie Evans, the deputy had said.

Mac's first instinct was to step forward and take credit where credit was due. But as much as he wanted to for more reasons than he cared to admit, he couldn't. He told himself there was no way Jill would believe that this Arnie was the man, would she?

He drove back to the houseboat. Who the hell was Arnie Evans, anyway? Mac had seen Jill's adverse reaction to the man—and his story. More importantly, why was the man lying? To save Jill? Or himself?

It didn't take Mac long at the Beach Bar to find out that Arnie Evans had supposedly been Trevor Forester's best friend. And that he had not only invested in the Inspiration Island development, he worked out there.

After a phone call to his cop buddy Charley Johnson, Mac found out that Arnie had run into some trouble with the law when he was younger. Twice he'd been picked up for having sex with underage girls. Both times he'd gotten off, supposedly because Trevor had paid off the parents of the girls.

Arnie had been one of the people the local sheriff had looked at in the cases of the missing teens. But they'd never been able to get anything on him.

Mac could feel himself getting deeper and deeper into Trevor Forester's murder. He started beating the bushes, looking for Shane, in a race against the clock. Come dark, he would be camped outside Jill Lawson's apartment—a dangerous place for him to be in more ways than one.

JILL COULDN'T RECALL a worse day.

Both Deputies Duncan and Samuelson seemed satisfied that Arnie Evans was her mystery lover— and her alibi for the time of the murder. As crazy as it seemed, she preferred being a suspect in Trevor Forester's murder than this.

After Arnie promised to go to the sheriff's department and make a statement, the deputies left. Duncan gave her an apologetic nod. Samuelson merely looked from Arnie to her and back, obviously disgusted that she'd made love with Trevor's best friend on the night her fiancé was murdered.

Samuelson didn't know the half of it. If Arnie was

telling the truth, she'd made love with a man she couldn't stand the sight of.

Her face burned with embarrassment as she watched the deputies leave. Finally she made herself look at Arnie. It was difficult. "Maybe they believe your story, but I don't."

"You sure hold a grudge a long time," Arnie said. "I think the reason I bugged you so much when were kids is that I just wanted you to notice me."

"Oh, I noticed you all right."

"I always liked you. It really ticked me off the way Trevor treated you." He sounded sincere. Then he got to his feet. "I should get going. I'm sorry if you're disappointed I was the man with you. I didn't mean to embarrass you. I had a feeling you wouldn't be happy about...us. I just couldn't let them hassle you anymore. And you were right, I did hear about that through my cousin. You know how news travels in this town."

Jill groaned. The whole town knew about her tryst in the lake cottage last night—and now they'd hear it was with Arnie.

"It'll blow over," he said as if reading her mind. "And don't worry. I won't bother you, considering how you feel about things...now."

She'd never seen this side of Arnie before. He was being much nicer than she ever would have guessed. Was it possible he really had been the man in the cottage?

It was that first kiss, she realized. The moment their lips had touched. That kiss had melted all her anger, resentment, fears about Trevor. She'd been seduced by a kiss. A kiss from Arnie Evans?

She cringed at the thought, even with him acting almost human. She just couldn't imagine him being the generous, loving man who'd transported her to another world and introduced her to passion. It had been more than sex. She had bonded with that man and now missed him, ached for him. And her heart and soul told her he wasn't Arnie Evans.

Arnie walked to the door and stopped. "I know Trevor could be a real jackass, but he was my best friend."

"Is that why you decided to give me an alibi?" she asked.

He shook his head, his dark gaze meeting hers. He really did seem shy around her without Trevor here. "I told the truth, Jill. I'm sorry, but it was me last night." He turned and started toward the door.

"Arnie?"

He stopped, his back to her.

"Did you know about the woman Trevor was seeing, Rachel?"

He didn't turn around. "I knew there was someone. I saw her driving your car once."

"Do you know her name?"

"Rachel. That's all I knew. But she never really mattered to Trevor. He was just stringing her along like he did all women."

He was planning to marry this one. "I appreciate you trying to help me," she said, feeling a little guilty. She swore she'd never have sex again.

Moments later she glanced out the window and

saw Arnie getting into a new black sports car—the same one that had been parked in front of the bakery this morning.

Why would Arnie be sitting across the street in his car at three-thirty in the morning watching her bakery? Was it possible he'd been considering telling her he was the man? Could she be wrong about him?

AFTER ARNIE LEFT, Jill called to get her locks replaced, remembering that someone had Trevor's key to her apartment. Brenna called just as she was getting ready to leave.

"Trevor never applied for a marriage license or got any blood tests and—are you ready for this?— he cashed in the second ticket, the one for Rachel Forester, the day *before* the party," Brenna said. "Either he changed his mind about marrying her, or he never planned to."

Maybe Arnie had been right about Trevor not caring about Rachel.

"I would say she had a great motive for murder if she found out," Brenna noted.

"No kidding." But what had she been looking for at the condo if not the ticket?

After they hung up, Jill changed clothes and drove out to meet with Alistair Forester, all the time thinking about motives for murder—and the other Scarlett. Was she Rachel?

The road to the Forester house was narrow and winding, providing glimpses of the lake through the cherry trees, some still heavy with fruit. Flathead cherries were famous and only grew on this side of the lake.

This early in the afternoon, the water was glassy smooth and green. The leaves of the cherry trees shimmered in the summer heat.

As the road narrowed even more along the rocky cliffs, Jill was reminded of the previous night when she'd been chasing her red Saturn. She'd thought it was Trevor driving her car. Instead, it must have been the other Scarlett.

As she parked the van, she caught sight of the cottage through the pine trees and felt a rush of emotion that had nothing to do with Arnie Evans. He couldn't have been the man, no matter what he said or how he acted or what evidence he was able to provide, she thought, remembering how she'd felt in the man's arms, the feelings he'd elicited from her.

The cottage seemed to pull her. She walked down to it and opened the door, peering inside. The deputies had already searched it. But still she had to look. Not that she knew what she was looking for.

The cottage was small. Just room enough for a bed, two club chairs, a small table and a bathroom. How had Arnie gotten the bra, she wondered, if he hadn't been the man? And what about the ring and her panties? Who had them?

She stood in the middle of the room. She could almost feel the man's presence, his touch such a clear memory her skin tingled and her body ached. She closed her eyes, sensing something of the man still there in the room, an intangible essence that assured her everything she believed about last night was true. Her lover was still masked, still a mystery, waiting to be found, wanting her as badly as she wanted him.

She opened her eyes. "Right. If he wants you so badly, where is he? Why hasn't he come looking for you? Why hasn't he come to your rescue?"

The only thing she could be sure of was that whoever the man had been last night, he'd stirred a desire in her she feared no other man could satisfy.

She started to leave, closing the door behind her, wishing she could close the door on last night as easily. The soles of her sandals scraped on something gritty on the floor. She looked down and saw what appeared to be mustard-colored dried mud on the threshold.

She bent and picked up a piece of it, surprised since she knew of no place around here that had mud that color. Crumbling it in her fingers, she had a flash of memory. She'd seen this kind of dried mud before. On Trevor's boots the last time he'd come into the bakery from the island!

ALISTAIR OPENED the door at Jill's knock. He looked ten years older, his face gray and drawn. Without a word, he hugged her.

"I am so sorry," Jill whispered.

He nodded wordlessly, his eyes shining with fresh tears as he led her to his den. "I had the maid make us some lemonade."

She wasn't thirsty but took the drink he offered her and sat down beside him on the sofa, wondering where Heddy was.

He seemed nervous, unsure, something totally alien for a man like him. "I know things weren't... good between you and my son."

She nodded. "I hadn't really seen Trevor lately. I had the feeling he'd been avoiding me. I wanted to believe it was just his work, but I think I knew better. I was going to break off the engagement last night, even before I found out there was someone else."

"Another woman," Alistair said.

"Yes. Did you know about her?"

He shook his head. "I'm sorry. You know how delighted I was that you were going to be part of our family. Trevor knew my sentiments, as well." His eyes filled with more tears. He squeezed her hand. "I am deeply saddened that you won't be my daughter-in-law."

She smiled. "Thank you."

"If there is anything you need, anything at all, please let me know," he said. "The funeral is tomorrow. Heddy insisted we open it up to the entire town. I think she needs to see a big turnout."

Jill nodded in understanding.

"We thought it was best to have it as soon as the coroner released the...body." His voice broke. "What did Trevor do that made someone want to kill him?"

Jill took Alistair's hand, knowing how hard this must be on him. How many women had Trevor been stringing along? Had one of them killed him?

"I hadn't seen Trevor much myself lately," Alistair said, composing himself. "Not since I cut him off financially." He nodded at Jill's surprise. "I know Trevor had planned to leave town last night. The sheriff said he'd purchased a second plane ticket. For a Mrs. Forester. A Rachel Forester. I told myself there must be some mistake."

Jill shook her head. There was no mistake. "There was a woman at the party dressed in the same costume I had on. It seems she planned to take my place once Trevor broke the news to me."

Alistair shook his head. "Despicable behavior. I am so ashamed." He closed his eyes as if he was in pain. "I'm so sorry."

"It's not your fault," she said.

He shook his head. "Yes, it is," he said opening his eyes again. "Heddy and I spoiled Trevor, and kept right on spoiling him. We gave him everything he ever asked for. Including that awful island. He wanted it so badly. As much as I disliked the idea, I thought he might make something of it. I thought it might...change him. Unfortunately his intent seems to have only been to swindle the people who trusted him, myself and the other investors. Inspiration Island indeed. I guess it was Trevor's little joke on us all."

"Who were the other investors?" Jill asked, suddenly wondering if one of the investors had found out about the swindle and killed Trevor.

Alistair named four people: Wesley Morgan, a local landowner; J. P. Davies, a retired computer whiz with a summer home on the lake—J.P. never spent more than a few weeks at the lake each year; and Arnie and Burt Evans.

Arnie's father invested in Inspiration Island? Burt Evans had owned a gas station in Polson, at the south end of the lake. He'd died in May from a heart attack, but Jill doubted he'd had much to invest. She'd always gotten the impression he'd barely scraped by.

"Trevor was much deeper in debt than I suspected," Alistair said. "Even if he had completed the island project, he couldn't have made enough to get himself out of debt and pay back the investors. Finishing the project is out of the question."

"What will happen to the island?" Jill asked.

"No one wanted that island before because of its history. Now its value is diminished because of the mess Trevor made out there," Alistair said.

How had Trevor made such a mess of things? She felt so sorry for Alistair. And Heddy. The woman must be beside herself. Trevor was her baby boy. He could do no wrong. "How is Heddy? This must be devastating for her on top of everything else."

"Your concern is touching," Heddy said sarcastically from the doorway, making them both turn in surprise.

Jill wondered how long Heddy had been standing there listening. Jill hurriedly stood and started toward the woman, but Heddy stopped her short.

"What are you doing here?" Heddy demanded.

Jill was taken aback. "Alistair asked me to—"

"I needed to talk to her about Trevor," Alistair said, pushing himself up from the couch.

"She never loved our son," Heddy accused, her eyes hard as stones as she glared at Jill. "I heard you say you weren't going to marry him. For all I know you killed him!''

"Heddy! Don't be ridiculous!" Alistair cried.

Heddy ignored him, her eyes like daggers. "This is all your fault, Jill. I told Alistair not to force Trevor into marrying you. 'Get yourself a nice girl. A girl like that Jill Lawson,' Heddy mimicked. "'Otherwise, you're not going to get a red cent of my money!' Isn't that what you told him, Alistair?''

"Heddy, for God's sake—"

"If you'd been half the woman Trevor needed, he wouldn't have gotten involved with that other woman and he'd be alive today," Heddy said angrily.

"No," Alistair said, taking his wife by the shoulders and turning her to face him. "Don't you dare blame this poor girl for our son's behavior. Don't you dare."

Heddy crumpled against him, sobbing in horrible gasps. Alistair held his wife to him, his eyes brimming with tears as he looked over Heddy's silver-blond head at Jill.

"I'm so sorry," Jill whispered.

Alistair closed his eyes.

Jill quietly slipped out, mortified by what she'd learned. Trevor had only asked her to marry him to please his father—and get the Forester money. Amazing that Trevor could still humiliate her even in death.

As she left, she wondered what Heddy had meant about Trevor being alive today if he hadn't gotten involved with that woman. The other Scarlett?

Chapter Seven

Jill's father's fishing boat was gone when she reached his house. She left him a note saying she had borrowed the ski boat and would be back soon.

The lake was a mirror, the late-afternoon sun hot as she hit the throttle and sped down the lake to the roar of the engine and the spray of the cool water.

She got her love of lakes from her father. He'd moved to Flathead Lake from Billings, bought the modest house on the lake and started an auto-parts business near Yellow Bay. He'd been successful and now, in his sixties, spent his days fishing on the lake. As the story went, her parents had both given up any hope of having children after years of trying when Jill had come along.

"It must have been the lake water," her father always joked. "Or maybe the good fishing. But your mother flourished here," he would say, and look at the lake with a kind of devotion. "We were blessed here. We got you."

So it was no wonder Jill loved the lake as much as her father. She'd grown up here and knew the lake well.

Except for what Trevor had named Inspiration Island. The island had always been off-limits. In the early days it had been owned by a wealthy recluse family. After the tragedies there, the island had been fenced and posted.

She'd heard rumors about there being deadly quicksand in places. Those rumors ran as rampant as the ones about the screams heard coming from the island some summer nights. Locals swore the place was haunted and avoided it.

Even her father, who was the most down-to-earth man she knew, always warned her to keep away from the island. He said that something about it frightened him. He never fished near it.

Given all that, she'd been surprised that, when the island had come up for sale, Trevor had talked Alistair into buying it and letting him develop it into an island resort.

The boat trip to the island took about thirty minutes from her father's place at the other end of the lake. Last night from the Foresters', which was closer, it would have taken more like ten, maybe fifteen minutes in the right boat.

Had that been Arnie who she thought got out of the boat at the Foresters' dock last night at eight-fifteen? Or had the man dressed as Rhett Butler been on the boat at all? She couldn't be sure. Once she'd seen the man go into the cottage, she hadn't noticed anyone else.

As she neared the island, she slowed the boat, a chill creeping over her at the sight of the old mansion sitting high on the cliffs at the island's north end. Weathered and dark, the stark frame of the empty structure could barely be seen through the pines, but there was just enough of it to disturb her.

While the other islands were dotted with cabins and expensive houses, boat docks and water toys strewn across the beaches, this island was just as it had been for decades.

She always avoided the island just as her father had and not because of the signs warning trespassers of prosecution.

It was the stories. Stories of a crazed young woman who'd been kept a prisoner there. According to local legend, Aria Hillinger had been the only daughter of Claude Hillinger and he'd treated her like a princess. But when she was in her teens, she realized she was a captive princess and she went mad.

She escaped once. When her father brought her back to the island, she was pregnant, according to the stories. Claude had delivered the baby himself so his daughter would never have to leave again.

At night Aria would stand on the fourth-floor balcony and cry for help. She was not even eighteen the day her father found her hanging from a rafter on the fourth-floor balcony overlooking the lake. Her child would have been five.

Claude killed himself when he found his daughter hanging there. He jumped from the balcony to the cliffs below. It was weeks before anyone found the two of them. By then, Aria's child was missing. Everyone speculated the child had either starved to death or drowned. Of course, some people said Aria had never escaped the island, not even once, and her baby had been Claude's, which was why she'd killed herself.

Some people still swore that on some still summer nights they could hear the woman's cries miles away.

Jill shivered and wondered why Trevor had thought anyone would want to live on this island again. As she glanced up at the weathered mansion, she also wondered why he hadn't torn down the old structure first thing.

She feared Trevor had planned to capitalize on the tragedies of this island. Why else would he leave that awful monstrosity standing? She could still see the old No Trespassing signs along the shore and pushed away thoughts of Claude Hillinger. If evil could survive, it did so here, she thought.

The largest cove on the east side sheltered a dock where two boats were moored. She slowed, pulled along one side of the dock and cut the engine. Grabbing the rope, she jumped out to tie it to a cleat, ignoring the large sign on the shore end of the dock: No Trespassing. Authorized Personnel Only.

She didn't recognize either of the boats, but she recognized the face that appeared at the construction-office window and quickly disappeared from view. Wesley Morgan, one of the investors.

She questioned why someone like Wesley would have invested in this island and then immediately knew the answer. Fast money. The only island left undeveloped in a beautiful Montana lake. Maybe it could have overcome its creepy past. Out-of-staters wouldn't know the history. All they would see was the beauty of the area.

As she neared the office, she thought about Trevor's big plans. High-end summerhouses. A marina. A four-star hotel and restaurant.

From what she could see, none of those plans had materialized. The small office was little more than a shed at the edge of the shore overlooking the dock. She could see no other buildings through the trees.

"Jill?" The voice behind her sounded surprised, maybe a little apprehensive. She turned, glad to see it was Wesley Morgan who came out of the office, not whoever owned the other boat.

Wesley was fiftysomething, slim, prematurely gray with a fatherly face. She watched him glance behind him as if he'd expected to see someone else come out of the office.

"What are you doing here?" Wesley asked, softening the words with a smile and, "Not that it isn't always nice to see you."

Uh-huh. "I wanted a look at the island."

He frowned. "There really isn't much to see."

She could believe that as she glanced toward several pieces of heavy equipment that had obviously been brought out by barge. A narrow dirt road snaked through the pines and disappeared, possibly the same road Claude Hillinger had once used to get to his mansion.

This did seem like a waste of time now that she was here. What had she hoped to find? Some yellow mud. But what would that prove? That the man she'd made love to had been on the island last night?

Or at least someone who'd gone into the cottage since last night had been on the island.

She glanced at the office, not ready to give up. "I'd love a tour," she said, and flashed him a smile.

Wesley looked more than surprised. "A tour? I'm not sure—"

"I really need to see this place." She glanced away. "I need to know why Trevor... I just need to see the island for myself."

Wesley looked as if he had better things to do, but finally he nodded and motioned toward a Jeep parked next to the office. "Hop in. Like I said, there isn't much to see."

As she walked along the side of the office, a shadow passed the window. She saw Wesley glance in that direction.

"Who's manning the office?" she asked as she climbed into the passenger side of the Jeep.

Wesley looked uncomfortable as he started the Jeep and backed out. "Nathaniel Pierce. Do you know him?"

She shook her head. But she knew him by reputation.

Wesley seemed to not want to say any more, but must have felt compelled to, given that she'd caught them both out here. "He might be interested in buying the island, but at this point, I don't want to jinx the deal—and he doesn't really want that made public."

She could understand now why Wesley was acting so secretive. Jill knew that if Nathaniel Pierce bought the island the investors would get at least

some of their money back. It was no secret Pierce
came from old family money.

"Why would he want the island?" she asked, really wondering more why Trevor had wanted it.

Wesley shook his head. "He says he wouldn't
develop it. Just let it go back to the way it's been
for years. I think he's worried about his view." He
shrugged at the whims of the rich. "His house over-
looks the island."

Wesley drove south along what was obviously a
newer narrow dirt road cut through the trees. The
island was only about a mile long and maybe half
a mile wide. Through the pines she would get
glimpses of the lake. The sun seemed to beat down
mercilessly on the island, and the air was eerily still
and dry. She yearned to be back in the boat on the
cool water and far from here.

"I'm surprised Trevor didn't get more done," she
said. Especially as he'd told her he'd been working
day and night for the past few months. Uh-huh.

Wesley didn't look away from his driving. "Bet
you're not as surprised as the investors."

"Trevor didn't let you come out here, either?"

Wesley shook his head. "He said he wanted to
surprise us. Even scheduled a Labor Day grand
opening to start selling lots for the next summer season." Wesley's voice was laced with bitterness.
"Oh, he surprised us all right."

The road ended abruptly at a gate with a sign that
read Restricted. No Admittance.

Wesley stopped and shifted down as he started to

turn onto an even narrower road that ran along the west side of the island.

To the south, through a tall, steel-mesh fence, Jill could see pines giving way to cattails, ferns and reeds. With a start, she noticed the tracks going through the gate. The road was rutted and muddy—the same odd mustard-colored mud she'd found in the cottage. The same mud she'd seen on Trevor's boots the last time she'd seen him.

"What's through there?" she asked, pointing at the gate.

"Swamp. The whole south end of the island is worthless, completely uninhabitable, and the north end is high cliffs and not much better. The engineering report that I saw...well, it glossed over some of the island's obvious problems as far as development went."

It sounded more and more like Trevor's only big plans for the island were to bilk the investors and skip town.

"That's a strange-colored mud," she commented. "I've never seen it anywhere else around the lake, have you?"

"No," he said. "Awful stuff. Like quicksand, it's so sticky and deep." Wesley released the clutch. The Jeep lurched up the west-side road.

Jill turned to look back through the fence. Quicksand? That must be why Trevor had gone to the trouble of fencing off the swamp. Seemed like a waste of money, though.

A man's face suddenly materialized out of the trees just beyond the fence.

"Wait!" she cried. "That man—"

Wesley hit the brakes and turned to look in the direction she indicated. "What man?"

She stared at the spot where she'd just seen the blond man from the bakery this morning. He was gone! How was that possible? He'd just been standing there. Where had he gone?

She kept looking. He had to still be there. He couldn't have moved that quickly. Unless he'd realized that she'd seen him and had some reason to hide.

"Didn't you say there wasn't anyone else on the island but Nathaniel Pierce and us?" she asked.

"There isn't. Who did you think you saw?"

She caught Wesley's pitying expression. Did he think she thought she saw Trevor? "I guess it was nothing."

"This must be hell for you," he said kindly.

She nodded. Trevor was definitely one reason she'd come out here today, but that wasn't the man she'd seen. She told herself she hadn't imagined him. But then again, she couldn't forget her reaction to him in the bakery this morning. It was so…odd.

Wesley got the Jeep going again.

She pretended to stare at the passing landscape. Wesley passed an area of scraped rocky earth that might have been cleared for a house. Who knew what Trevor had planned? A few stakes with small red flags on them fluttered in the breeze around the perimeter of the spot.

Why had Trevor bothered if he'd always planned to run out on the investors—and her? Maybe he really had been serious about Inspiration Island at some point. Maybe before the other Scarlett came along. Is that what his mother had meant?

Near the shoreline she spotted more wooden stakes, more red flags moving restlessly in the breeze.

Wesley drove over a rise near the north end of the island and the rear of the mansion appeared out of the pines. The heat pressed down on her and for a moment she couldn't breathe.

"That's where they found Trevor's boat," Wesley said, pointing off to the west.

She could feel Wesley watching her, expecting what reaction? she wondered.

"Who found him?" she asked even though Brenna had already told her.

"A fisherman noticed the boat as he was passing the island but didn't see anyone inside, so he went over to check."

It seemed strange that Trevor had been killed within view of the island. Within view of the mansion people around the area swore was haunted.

She felt a chill as Wesley drove on past the mansion, back through the pines to the office.

"Anything else?" he asked as he parked in the patch of shade beside the small wooden office.

"Do you know anyone named Rachel?" She watched his face. "She was a friend of Trevor's."

He frowned. "Rachel? No, sorry."

She nodded. "Thanks for showing me around," she said, climbing out of the Jeep. He followed her around to the front of the office.

"Can I ask you one more thing?" she said before he went back inside. She could see that only Wesley's boat remained at the dock. Nathaniel Pierce must have decided not to wait. She hoped her showing up here hadn't made him rush off or change his mind about buying the island. "Did you lose a lot of money in this project?"

Wesley looked toward the lake. "Just my life's savings."

"I'm sorry. I suppose you heard that Trevor was planning to leave the country?"

He raked a hand through his hair, his features taut with anger. "No. When was he leaving?"

"The night of the party."

Wesley looked over at her. "You weren't going with him?"

She shook her head. "Thanks again for the tour." As she started down the slope to the dock, she thought about the three investors. She doubted J.P. was worried about any money he'd put into the project, since the last she'd heard he was worth billions. And Arnie's father, Burt, couldn't have invested much since he didn't have much to begin with.

That left Wesley Morgan. He had the most to lose—and that gave him a motive for Trevor's murder, she realized with a start.

She found herself hurrying, but not because she feared Wesley. She just wanted off this island. It felt cursed. And Trevor's murder seemed to prove it.

But as she got into the boat, started the engine and pulled away from the island, she thought about the man she'd seen in the trees at the south end of the island. The blond man from the bakery that morning.

Instead of turning her boat home, she motored slowly toward the southern, marshy end of the island, staying close to the shore. This end of the lake was shallow and full of weeds.

An enormous flock of pelicans floated overhead, and she could see ducks and geese in pockets of water in the marshy area before the bushes and trees began. She cut the engine and let the boat drift as she neared the far-south end of the island.

A flash of silver caught her eye. A small fishing boat was tied up under some bushes. She picked up the emergency paddle her father kept on board and maneuvered her boat under the limbs of a clump of bushes in a small cove—a spot just far enough away that when whoever owned the fishing boat returned, neither she nor her boat could be seen. But she could see him.

She didn't have to wait long.

The man she'd seen earlier behind the restricted area, the same one who'd come into the bakery that morning, appeared from behind the bushes. He was carrying a small navy duffel bag. The bottom of the bag, which was thick with the mustard-yellow mud from behind the restricted area, sagged under the weight of whatever was inside.

He put the bag carefully down in the bow, then untied the bow rope from a branch, shoved out the craft and jumped in. His boat motor spurted to life an instant later.

She watched him angle away, heading west. He

was going along the far side of the island, the side opposite from the office. So no one would see him?

She waited, then eased her boat out of the cove with the paddle, moving along the edge of the bushes until she could see him again. A little farther up the lake in the shallows was a favorite spot for lake-trout fishing. He headed for that as if it had been his destination all along. But he didn't stop to fish. He kept going until he was past the island. Past the spot where Trevor's boat had been found with his body inside.

The man turned once to look back at the island, then he hit the throttle and headed north up the lake.

What was in the bag he'd brought out of the restricted area of the island? And who was he?

She remembered her reaction to him in the bakery that morning. That instant when she'd seen him in the trees. And his shock of recognition just before he'd ducked out of sight.

The sun had dropped behind the mountains, leaving the lake's surface bathed in gold.

Jill waited, hanging back, then she followed him.

Chapter Eight

Jill watched from a distance as the man tied up the fishing boat to the stern of a houseboat docked at the far end of the marina and disappeared inside it. He'd left the duffel bag in the fishing boat, but she knew there was no way to get a look at the contents until after dark.

In the long, cool shadows of the pines stretching out over the water, she pulled her boat up on shore and walked toward the Bandit's Bay Marina office. The fading sunset streaked the lake's surface like oil. She could hear music coming from the jukebox at the Beach Bar, the sound of children splashing in the swimming area, the drone of a motorboat crossing the lake.

As she stepped into the marina office, she kept her eye on the houseboat, afraid he would come out and see her and know she'd followed him.

"Well, hello!"

Jill turned to see Brenna behind the marina-office counter.

"Mom bribed me with dinner if I'd come by and help," Brenna said, coming around the counter to give Jill a hug. "She's making her famous barbecued pork ribs. She would love it if you could stay for dinner."

"Thanks, but I really can't." Especially tonight. She smiled at her friend. Brenna was as sweet as she was pretty and smart. She could have been anything, but she'd opted to go into journalism, got a job at the local paper and stuck around Bigfork to help her family at the marina in her spare time.

"How are you doing?" Brenna asked, studying Jill.

"Okay."

"I'm still trying to find out more about this Rachel person for you," Brenna said. "It would help if we had a last name."

Jill nodded, hating to ask. "I have another favor."

"Sure."

"I need to know who owns that houseboat tied up at the far end of the docks," she said.

"The one down in the old slips?"

Jill nodded.

"Does this have anything to do with Trevor's murder?"

"Possibly."

Brenna flipped through the file and pulled out a card. "Mackenzie Cooper. Listed a post-office box in Whitefish as permanent address."

"I wonder what he's doing here?"

She looked up from the card. "Fishing, I would imagine. Speaking of fishing—"

"I saw him out on the island earlier and I got the impression he didn't want to be seen."

"You went out to the island? Oh, you couldn't get me near that place. I can't believe you went out there by yourself."

"Wesley was there." She didn't mention Nathaniel Pierce. Not even to Brenna. "The place is way creepy. Especially the south end where I saw this Mackenzie Cooper guy."

"Jill, if you think he knows something about Trevor's murder, you should call the sheriff."

"All the man's done so far is trespass. I want to do some checking on him first."

"I can put him in the computer as soon as I get home," Brenna promised. "Want me to call you if I come up with anything, if it isn't too late?"

"Even if it's late. You don't know anything about him?"

Brenna shook her head. "He really keeps to himself. Except I have seen him go to the Beach Bar. Usually in the evening just before dark. He doesn't stay long. Has a beer and walks back to his boat. I'd say he was lonely, except he doesn't look like the lonely type."

Jill nodded. Mackenzie Cooper had no reason to be lonely—unless he chose to be.

"He's really good-looking."

"I suppose so." Jill felt her cheeks flush. "You wouldn't be interested in having a beer later, after dinner, at the Beach Bar, would you?"

Brenna smiled. "I'd love to have a beer with you— Oh, no, you don't."

"I just need you to detain him as long as you

can,'' Jill said quickly. "Buy him a beer. He can't say no, right?"

"Wrong. What are you planning to do?"

"It's probably better if you don't know."

Brenna groaned. "Tell me you aren't going aboard his boat."

"Okay, I'm not going aboard." She quickly hugged her friend. "I really appreciate this."

"What if I can't keep him in the bar long enough?" Brenna asked, sounding scared. "We need some kind of signal so you'll know he's coming back to his boat. I could ring the bell down at the gas docks. It isn't very loud, though."

"That's perfect." Jill smiled. "You're the best."

"Just be careful. I'd feel a lot better if Trevor's killer was behind bars and we knew more about this Mackenzie Cooper."

Wouldn't they all? Jill thought as she returned the ski boat to her father's dock. His car was in the driveway, but his fishing boat was still gone. Gary fished most days until dark. She wondered if he was alone. She'd heard he'd been playing a lot of bingo lately with one of the ladies from the seniors center and that the woman liked to fish.

On the drive to her apartment, Jill thought about the idea of her father remarrying. It had been four years since her mother had died. Still, it seemed too soon for her father to have found someone else. Jill knew she was being selfish, but she couldn't help it.

Didn't she want to see her father find love again? As if it was that easy to find it even once, let alone twice in a lifetime.

A cool breeze stirred the large poplar tree next to her bakery as she parked the van and got out. She had enough time to get something to eat and change clothes.

She glanced down the street and saw Arnie's black sports car. Her stomach clenched at the sight. He was the last person she wanted to see. It had been a long day, and she was tired and hungry and in no mood for him.

But the car appeared to be empty. Maybe he was at the video store down the block or one of the restaurants along the main drag.

She climbed the back steps to her apartment, her thoughts returning to the island and the man she'd seen. Mackenzie Cooper. What had he carried off the island in that duffel bag?

As she started to open the apartment door with her key, she stopped, momentarily confused to find the door already slightly ajar. Beyond it, she could hear someone inside her apartment. Not again!

She started to turn back down the stairs, intending to go out to her van and call the sheriff's department from her cell phone, when she heard Arnie's voice.

Cautiously she pushed open the door and peered in. The bedroom door was open and she could see Arnie digging through one of her kitchen drawers as if looking for something. He was talking to himself, although she couldn't make out the words.

"What are you doing?" she demanded, stepping into the apartment.

He looked up, startled to see her, his eyes narrowing for a moment before he grinned sheepishly.

"You caught me," he said, and closed the drawer. "I was looking for a pen to leave you a note."

It was an obvious lie. He'd been searching the back of the drawer as if looking for something other than a pen. "How did you get in here?"

"I just changed all of your locks," he said. "Oh, you didn't know I moonlight for Doug's Key and Safe?"

No, she hadn't known that when she'd called them. But then, Doug's was the only locksmith in town.

Arnie held out her new keys. "That's why I was leaving you the note. The larger key fits the front door of the bakery, the smaller one the back door. You get two keys each, but you should probably make at least one spare."

She took the keys he handed her. "How many spares did you make?"

He looked insulted. "You really don't trust me, do you."

"Should I?"

"Yes. I'm sorry I was such a jerk when we were kids. But you've never made the effort to get to know me since we've been adults."

"Can you blame me?"

He seemed to consider that. "No, I guess not." He smiled. "Sorry if I scared you. I wanted to make sure you had new locks before tonight."

"Thanks." He was making her feel like a real bitch.

He started toward the door, then stopped. "Do you have any idea who might have killed Trevor?"

The question took her by surprise. "No. Do you?"

He shook his head.

"Did you know it was Alistair's idea that Trevor marry me?" she asked, not realizing she was going to.

Arnie looked away.

"So you did know." Everyone had known but her.

"Trevor was…" He waved a hand, looked at the floor, then at her. "I know how he was, but I miss him." He shrugged. "He and I were close, you know?"

She nodded, feeling the need to say something. "He always said you were his best friend."

Arnie smiled. "Thanks."

Maybe Arnie Evans was right. Maybe she didn't know him. And maybe he wasn't such a bad guy, after all.

"There is one more thing," Arnie said slowly. He looked embarrassed, unsure. "Trevor had something of mine. An IOU from an old gambling debt. If you run across it…"

So that was what he'd been looking for.

"I'll call you and let you know, but I haven't seen it," she said. How like Trevor to hold Arnie to a gambling debt.

"I knew you'd give it to me if you found it." Arnie stepped toward her until he was only an arm's length away. His dark eyes bored into hers as he looked down at her. "I wish I could change the past," he said, his voice little more than a whisper.

Then, before she could react, he grabbed her upper arms, pulled her to him and kissed her. His kiss was hard and wet, his tongue forcing her lips apart, plundering her surprised mouth.

Then just as suddenly, he let go of her and stepped back, seeming surprised and embarrassed by his impetuousness. "I'm sorry. I just..." He stumbled backward to the door and then was gone.

Jill stared after him for a moment before she hurried to the door, closed and locked it. Leaning against it, she wiped her mouth with her hand, wanting to scrub the taste of him from her and at the same time wanting to rejoice.

Arnie Evans had not been the man in the cottage last night! She wanted to shout it from the rooftop.

Her buoyant mood fell like a lead balloon. When she told the deputies, she'd destroy her alibi.

Not just hers, but Arnie's. So why had he lied? Was he just trying to help her—or was he the one who really needed the alibi?

She closed her eyes and rubbed her temples. She needed to shower and brush her teeth to banish every trace of Arnie Evans. The fact that he hadn't been her lover still cheered her to no end. She'd known in her heart he wasn't the man. She'd known!

But what had he really been looking for when she'd come into the apartment? An IOU? Or something else?

She opened her eyes and pushed away from the door when something crunched under the sole of her shoe. Looking down, she spotted the dried yellow mud on her floor. It must have come from Arnie's work boots, because she'd cleaned the apartment this morning after it had been ransacked last night.

Arnie had been in the restricted area of the island!

What was behind that steel fence that had recently attracted so many people there?

She had no idea, but she was going to find out. The sun was down and soon she'd find out what Mackenzie Cooper had brought out of the restricted area in his duffel bag.

JILL WAITED in the cool shadows of the pines at the edge of the water until she saw Mackenzie Cooper leave his houseboat and walk up to the Beach Bar, just as Brenna said he did every evening.

The Beach Bar was a classic Montana bar with silver dollars, elk antlers and stuffed lake trout on the walls. Brenna's family had built the bar at the end of the pier on pilings so that it overlooked the marina resort. One whole side was open to the air with stools and a few tables.

It was where both locals and tourists hung out, one of the few bars on the water and definitely blue-collar and fishermen friendly. Country-and-western music throbbed from the jukebox, blending with the sound of voices and the lap of water against the docks.

Jill waited until Mackenzie Cooper was well on his way to the bar before she slipped out of the pines and headed for the houseboat tied at the farthest dock from the marina, about thirty yards offshore.

She'd known she wouldn't be able to just walk down the dock to the boat without being seen. That left only one way out to the houseboat with any hope of going undetected. Swim.

No light glowed inside the houseboat as she waded into the dark water. She couldn't be sure that Brenna would be able to keep him at the bar. Jill couldn't even be sure that tonight he wouldn't change his routine, cut the evening short and return before she'd had time to search the houseboat and get away again.

She took a deep breath. She'd worn a shortie wet suit and a waterproof bag clipped to her waist with what she could find for tools to break into the boat. The water chilled her exposed skin as she dived under the surface. The small dry bag at her waist slowed her as she began to swim underwater through the open area to the docks.

She needed to stay under to keep from being seen for as long as she could. Once she reached the docks, she could swim alongside them to the houseboat.

Her pulse pounded in her ears, beating faster at just the thought of what she'd find in the duffel bag.

She tried to gauge her distance. If she surfaced too soon, she could be spotted from the bar. If she didn't surface soon enough, she'd come up under the docks.

Her pulse spiked when she thought of being caught under a dock again. When she was nine, she and a neighbor boy had been playing and decided to hide under the dock at her house. She'd gotten her suit caught on a nail.

She released a little of her held breath now, swimming through the cold darkness, calculating in her head how far she'd come, how much farther she had to go and trying not to remember that day so many years ago when she was trapped under the dock.

She was already running out of air, her growing panic stealing too much oxygen, stealing too much of the time she would be able to stay underwater. Something brushed her bare leg. Just weeds, she knew, but her panic, her fear fueled by the memory of almost drowning all those years ago, took over.

She surfaced in a rush, gasping for air, surprised by how far she still was from the docks and the houseboat. She shot a look toward the bar. She could see Mackenzie Cooper sitting on a stool, boot heels hooked on the rung, a beer bottle in his hand, a lazy look on his face, all his focus on the woman before him. Brenna. Thank heaven for Brenna.

Diving beneath the surface again, Jill swam toward the docks, more aware of the distance yet spurred on by a need to see what the man had found on the island today.

At last, she reached the docks and surfaced, then swam alongside to the houseboat and climbed the short ladder onto the deck. She stood dripping and trying to catch her breath as she heard the distinct sound of footsteps on the dock headed her way. Was it possible he was already coming back? That Brenna had rung the bell while Jill was underwater?

Jill placed a hand over her thumping heart as she realized there was more than one person coming down the dock. She could hear the voices, the clink of ice in glasses and the sound of laughter.

Peeking around the bow of the houseboat, Jill saw four people headed for a sailboat in a slip about fifty yards away. Mackenzie Cooper's boat was isolated from any of the other boats. She suspected that was the way he wanted it, which made her all the more suspicious.

The people boarded the sailboat, laughing and talking loudly, and Jill pulled the penlight from the dry bag at her waist and crept back to the stern of the houseboat where the small fishing boat had been tied.

Shining the light into the bottom of the fishing boat, she saw that the duffel bag wasn't still there. But then, she hadn't expected it to be. She'd noticed the way he'd carried the duffel, the way he'd laid it carefully in the bow of his fishing boat. Whatever he'd found in the restricted area of the island, it was something valuable, something too valuable to leave out in the fishing boat.

Keeping to the shadow of the houseboat, she moved across the stern to the back entrance. To her surprise the door wasn't locked. He must have figured he could see the boat from the bar and wasn't worried anyone would bother with it.

Carefully she slid open the screen door and slipped in, glad she wouldn't have to use the makeshift breaking-and-entering tools she'd brought from the bakery. Technically, then, she wasn't breaking and entering, right? She didn't close the screen. Just in case she needed to make a fast getaway.

It was dark in the houseboat, the curtains on the windows drawn. She swept the beam of the penlight across the cabin. The inside of the boat was modestly furnished, clean and uncluttered.

Was there a Mrs. Cooper? Jill didn't think so. No feminine touches anywhere that she could see. She quickly went through the boat. It didn't take long. One bedroom. Bed made. Bedding in the storage compartment under it. Bureau drawers, neat. Not a lot of clothing. Nothing fancy.

Lots of books, worn classics. A man who read. In the living area, she found more books, stereo, TV, VCR. Some storage.

She still hadn't found the duffel bag. She went into the small kitchen-dining room and looked in the cupboards. He had a lot of spices and staples, well-worn cookbooks, a well-stocked pantry and fridge. He must like to cook. That, of course, appealed to her.

No navy duffel. Could he have gotten rid of it between the time she'd left and returned?

She saw something through the bedroom doorway that made her heart jump. The closet door stood open. She'd been so busy looking for the duffel that she'd given the clothes hanging in his closet only a cursory glance, her attention more on the floor under them.

But now her gaze settled on something dark, something familiar.

She moved toward the open closet like a sleepwalker. Even before she touched the fabric, she caught the faint hint of her perfume still in the weave. As she stared at the Rhett Butler costume,

her pulse pounded so hard she almost didn't hear
the bell ring down at the gas dock.

Now more than ever she needed to find the duffel
bag. She had to know what this man was doing on
the island. What he was doing in the cottage last
night.

Her hands were shaking as she looked around the
boat, frantically trying to see if there was some hiding place she'd overlooked. She glanced at her
watch. She had a few minutes. Three at the most
before he reached the boat.

The duffel wasn't in the boat. She'd looked ev-
erywhere. As she moved toward the open doorway
at the stern, she spotted a storage compartment she
hadn't noticed before. She rushed to it, unlatched
the door and shone the penlight inside.

It was deep, so deep she realized it must have
another opening out on the deck. All she could see
from this vantage point was the side of an orange
plastic crate.

She hurried out the door to find she'd been right.
There was another opening to the compartment. She
lifted the hatch.

Her heart leaped at the sight of the navy duffel
bag. Any moment now she would hear his footfalls
on the old wooden dock.

Her pulse pounded as she reached for the duffel,
then stopped. The bag sat on top of the plastic crate,
and under it she could see an old anchor, some worn
rubber boots, an assortment of old gloves. The zipper on the bag was open a few inches.

Maybe she'd been wrong about the value of the

contents, she thought as she stared at the mud-encrusted duffel bag. She glanced at her watch. Time was up!

Hurriedly, she unzipped the bag fully, now expecting to find rocks or driftwood, and shone the beam of the penlight inside. Her chest tightened as the beam skittered over what appeared to be a volleyball-size clod of that distinctive mustard mud from the restricted area of the island.

The beam stilled on a dark place in the dried mud. A hole. No, not a hole—she moved the light—two eye sockets! A skull! A human skull! The scream caught in her throat as she heard the creak of a heavy step on the deck behind her.

Chapter Nine

Mac had hoped for news of Shane at the bar. Instead, the daughter of the owner of the marina had bought him a beer. She was attractive and nice, but had seemed nervous in her attempt to make small talk.

He'd downed the beer quickly, not sure exactly what she'd been hoping for. Whatever it was, it wasn't happening.

He'd left a lot of messages around town, but still nothing from Shane. Now he was just anxious to grab what he needed and head for Jill's apartment, where he would spend the night making sure she was safe.

It was his own fault for getting involved with her. Once he found Shane and returned the coins to Pierce, he told himself, she would be safe. Then he would pack up and leave Flathead Lake earlier than he'd planned, even though summer wasn't quite over.

Change of plans. Thanks to that one instant in time when he'd kissed Jill Lawson.

As he neared the houseboat, he heard a scuffling

sound and tensed. It was growing dark now, but he could see movement in the shadows by his houseboat. His pace quickened.

He was within yards of the boat when he saw what appeared to be two figures fighting. A man in a black ski mask and a woman in a wet suit. The man struck the woman and she slumped in his arms just an instant before the man spotted Mac running down the docks toward him.

Mac saw at once what the man was about to do and knew there was nothing he could do to stop him. In one swift movement, the man threw the unconscious woman over the side of the boat. She hit the water with a splash and went under. Then the man ran the length of the dock and dived into the lake, disappearing into the darkness and water as Mac raced toward the spot where he'd seen the woman go under.

He dived in. The water was shockingly cold, as well as dark and murky, but fortunately not deep. He brushed her arm and quickly made contact with her rubber-clad body and dragged her to the surface and up onto the dock.

As he laid her down on the dock and brushed her long dark hair from her face, he let out a curse. Jill Lawson. Quickly he leaned down to see if she was still breathing. What the hell had she been doing on his boat?

He started to give her mouth-to-mouth resuscitation, but the moment his mouth touched hers, she let out a gasp, her eyes flying open. She looked surprised, scared, confused, all at once. Then she coughed and tried to sit up.

"Are you all right?" he asked as he helped her into a sitting position.

She coughed a few more times, then looked around as if she wasn't sure where she was. She was shaking either from fear or the cold. Or both.

He lifted her into his arms and carried her into the houseboat. Her teeth chattered as he took her into the bathroom, sat her on the closed lid of the toilet and reached in to get the shower going.

"Wh-what are you d-doing?" she stammered.

"Getting you warmed up."

Something flickered in her gaze.

"Can you get out of that wet suit by yourself?"

She made a determined try, but she was shaking too hard. He turned her around and unzipped the back, revealing a strong, bare tanned back and a small, red string bikini. This woman was going to be the death of him.

The moment she felt the zipper stop, she was working at the sleeves, trying to pull them from her arms, struggling without much success as she said, "I can get it."

"Uh-huh. Here." He slipped the sleeve from her arm. She clutched the neoprene to her chest with a modesty that made him smile. He knew every wonderful inch of that body. "Let me help you. I'll close my eyes."

He dragged the wet-suit sleeve from her other arm, then—closing his eyes more for his protection than hers—pulled the neoprene down her slim body.

The wet suit fit like a glove and sucked down over her contours like a second skin. He peeled the rubbery material down her legs to her feet.

She rested a hand on his shoulder for balance as he tugged the wet suit off her feet.

Then, the wet suit in hand and his eyes still closed, he rose slowly to a standing position. "Will you be all right in the shower alone?"

"I'll be fine," she said, sounding a little breathless, her teeth still chattering.

"Okay. I'll be just outside the door if you need me." He turned his back to her, opened his eyes and left with the dripping wet suit. He went out on the deck, needing the cool air, and sucked in several breaths. He hung the suit over the railing to dry and listened for her. He could hear the shower running.

He worried she might pass out and fall. But he heard no alarming thumps, just the water running. He was still shaken from how close she'd come to getting killed.

He swore, angry with himself. Angry with her— what was she doing here, anyway? Angry that he'd let the bad guy get away. He told himself that protecting Jill Lawson wasn't his job. His job was finding Pierce's coins. But he knew he was only telling himself that because he'd failed at both.

He had to get this woman out of his hair, out of his mind, and soon. The shower stopped.

He started to go back inside, but spotted something on the deck. A penlight and a small, dark dry bag. He picked up both. In the dry bag, he found bakery tools and smiled in spite of himself. It appeared Jill Lawson had intended to break into his houseboat with a spatula.

He stepped back inside and looked up as she came out of the bedroom, her face flushed from the shower. She was wearing one of his shirts, a pale-blue chambray. Behind her he could see the wet string bikini on his towel bar.

She stopped when she saw him and looked ill at ease even though his shirt hung down to her knees, more than covering her. She plucked the fabric away from her breasts with her right hand, making him keenly aware that she wore nothing under the shirt. Her other hand was down at her side, hidden behind the folds of the shirt, but all he could think about was the body he knew so well beneath those folds.

Her long, golden-brown hair was pulled up off her neck, wet tendrils curling at her temples and framing her lightly freckled face.

His chest constricted. God, she was something! She smelled of his soap and a heat that wasn't all from the shower. He'd never wanted a woman more than he wanted her right now.

She raised her chin and met his gaze. His knees almost buckled. He stepped to her, lost in those big brown eyes and the chemistry shooting like sparks between them. His hand cupped the nape of her neck. Gently, he pulled her to him. His gaze dropped to her full mouth, the lips slightly parted. Lost. He was completely lost.

He breathed her in as he dropped his mouth to hers. She tasted just as he remembered. Sweet, warm, wet—

He froze when he felt cold steel jab into his ribs. His pistol. He'd left it beside the bed before he went to the bar.

"Who are you?" she asked, sounding scared.

"My name's Mackenzie Cooper." Carefully he removed his hand from her neck and stepped back, concerned in her current state she just might shoot him. From the way she held the gun, she'd used one before. Just his luck. If she pulled the trigger, it wouldn't be an accident.

"I know your name," she said. "Who *are* you?"

"I'm a private investigator. Want to tell me what you were doing on my boat?"

"I followed you from the island. I know you were behind the restricted area. I know there was a human skull in the duffel bag you brought out of there."

He tried not to show his surprise. "I see." He glanced toward the compartment where he'd put the duffel earlier. The door was closed and the man who'd attacked her hadn't taken it—he'd had nothing in his hands when he'd dived into the water.

"How's your head?" he asked. "I think I have some aspirin."

"My head's fine. So you're a private investigator." She frowned. "Were you investigating last night at the Forester party?"

He glanced toward the closet. The door was open and that damned costume was right where he'd hung it. He should have burned it, but he hadn't been able to. So much for sentimental value. "Why don't you put the gun down and we can talk about this."

She kept the weapon trained on him. "Were you investigating in the cottage last night?"

He flinched. She'd finally gotten to the heart of it.

"I found the Rhett Butler costume in your closet," she said, "with these in the right-hand pocket." She pulled out her black panties and dangled them before him.

He swore under his breath. She'd think he was some kind of pervert.

"I'd like my engagement ring back," she said. "I assume you picked it up, too."

He met her gaze. "I don't have it."

She lifted a brow. "Then maybe Arnie has it. Maybe he's the one I remember from the cottage, after all."

Ouch, that hurt. "One of us was definitely a lucky man," he said, then wished he'd bitten his tongue.

Anger flashed in her eyes. "You're lucky I don't shoot you. When you were in the bakery this morning, you could have told me who you were. You saw the deputies there. I know you overheard what was being said, and you knew I needed an alibi for the time of Trevor's murder."

He nodded. He might be a lot of things, but he wasn't a liar. At least not about this.

"They didn't believe my lame excuse about a man in the cottage seducing me."

Who had seduced whom? He wasn't sure.

Her voice rose with her anger. "Or you could have said something when Arnie Evans came in and announced that he had been my mystery lover."

"Did you believe him?" Mac had to ask.

"No."

He knew he shouldn't have taken so much satisfaction in that. "I wouldn't have let you go to jail."

She shook her head, obviously disgusted with him, but not as disgusted as he was with himself.

"I'm sorry," he added, "but I had my reasons."

Her eyes narrowed and he could see that if she had even an ounce of killer's instinct in her, she would have pulled the trigger. He watched her reach for his cell phone on the coffee table where he'd tossed it earlier.

"I'm sure you also have a good reason why you were at the Foresters' party last night dressed in the same costume Trevor was planning to wear," she said. "And an even better reason why you haven't told the sheriff you were with me in the cottage."

She picked up the phone and hit three numbers. He put his money on 911. "Not to mention the human skull you have in your duffel bag."

"Hang up."

She put the phone to her ear.

"*Hang up.* Please."

She glared at him for a moment, then hit the off button, but still kept the weapon trained on him. He considered taking it away from her, but decided it would only make matters worse. Somehow he had to convince her to stay out of this.

"I do have a good reason for being at the party last night," he said. As for what had happened in the cottage…well, he could explain gravity better than he could that.

He turned his back on her and walked into the small galley kitchen. He knew Jill Lawson wasn't the kind of woman to shoot a man in the back— even if she didn't. "I need a beer. You want one?" She didn't answer, so he pulled two long-necks out of the fridge, walked back into the living room, twisted off the top of one and held it out to her.

When she didn't take it, he set the beer on the coffee table next to where she stood, then sat down in a chair facing her and twisted the cap off his own beer. He took a swig, studying her, trying to decide the best way to handle her. And handle her, literally, was exactly what he wanted to do. But then, that was what had gotten him into this mess.

"Trevor Forester called me the day before the party," he said after a moment. "He'd heard I was a private investigator and wanted to hire me."

"Hire *you?*" she said, suspicion in her tone as she glanced around the houseboat.

"There aren't many private investigators in Bigfork. I actually have an office in Whitefish." He didn't know why he was explaining himself. Maybe because he wanted her to know he was legit. "Trevor said he feared his life was in danger."

Her eyes widened and she lowered herself into the chair next to the coffee table. She rested the weapon on her thigh and reached for the beer with her free hand. She took a sip, watching him over the bottle.

"Trevor said he needed to talk to me in person, but couldn't until the next evening," Mac continued. "I was to meet him at the party, or more precisely, in the lake cottage at eight-fifteen. He had a costume delivered to the marina for me with instructions that I was to go straight to the cottage via the shore and be inconspicuous.''

"Inconspicuous as Rhett Butler?"

"I had no idea he planned to show up in the same costume. Or that you would mistake me for him."

Her eyes narrowed. "You were the one who kissed *me* the instant I stepped into the cottage."

"I did it to shut you up. I saw a boat approaching. I wasn't sure who was on board." A small lie, but he didn't want to bring up Nathaniel Pierce. "I figured Trevor had his reasons for such a clandestine meeting—and his reasons for believing his life was in danger. I didn't want you giving me away."

"So that was all there was to it," she said.

He knew she was waiting for him to tell her that there was a hell of a lot more to the part where they'd made love.

He looked her in the eye, knowing how important it was that he make her believe him. "We just got a little carried away, I guess. Pretty hot sex. Must have been the intrigue of it. I'm sure we'd be disappointed if we tried it again."

The hurt in her eyes was almost his undoing. He feared, though, that he was right. They would be disappointed. Last night had been…amazing. He also feared the reverse—that making love to her would be even better the second time—and that he'd be tempted to love. Again.

He cursed himself for hurting her, but it would be much worse to let her think anything was going to

come out of last night's lovemaking. It would serve
no purpose to tell her he'd never felt anything like
what they'd shared. Even if they'd ended up making
love again a few minutes ago before she pulled the
gun on him, it wouldn't have changed the final out-
come—which was him leaving. Soon.

He was a loner, a guy who never stayed in one
place long, and he liked it that way. Jill Lawson was
a woman with deep roots, a woman who, until a
couple of days ago, was engaged to be married.

"Now you know my reasons for not telling the
deputies I was with you in the cottage. I didn't want
to get involved in Trevor's murder."

OH, SHE UNDERSTOOD all right. He didn't want to
get involved with the authorities—or with her. It
was just a one-night stand.

So why didn't she believe him? Not his supposed
nonchalance about their lovemaking last night or his
refusal to become involved in Trevor's murder.

"If you didn't want to get involved, then what
were you doing out on the island today, Mackenzie?"

He took a swallow of beer. "I was curious. And
you can call me Mac."

Mac. "I saw the skull in the duffel bag, Mac,"
she reminded him.

He shrugged. "There's an old cemetery on the
island. Probably early pioneers. That's not that un-
usual."

"And it interests you because…?"

He shrugged. "I was just curious what was be-hind that restricted fence. Weren't you?"

"I still am. I know Trevor and Arnie Evans have been in there working. I've seen the mud on their boots."

Mac nodded. "They were probably trying to get rid of the bodies before anyone found out. If there are any relatives of those pioneers still around, they could make a stink about the bodies being moved. Even shut down construction, possibly."

She stared at him, wishing she could find a flaw in his logic. He seemed to have all the answers.

She couldn't help being disappointed the skull hadn't meant more. And angry with him for making it sound as if their lovemaking had been...what? Great sex but a fluke?

"Where is the skull?" he asked.

"Still in the duffel, unless whoever jumped me took it."

He shook his head. "He didn't have it when he dived into the water."

"I wonder what he was after," she said, watching Mac, curious how he would explain this away.

"You."

"Me?"

"I imagine he followed you here."

She couldn't believe this. "Why?"

"Trevor owed a lot of people, people who might think that because you were his fiancée, you were in on scamming them."

She hadn't thought of that. "I think the man was the same one who was in my apartment last night.

He demanded my engagement ring and was upset when I told him I didn't have it.'' She noticed Mac's surprise. "He tore the silver bracelet that Trevor gave me from my wrist.''

"Did he take any of your other jewelry?''

She shook her head. "You think it was someone who knew Trevor had given me the ring and the bracelet? The bracelet was just a trinket, not worth anything.''

Mac took another swallow of beer. "The word around the area is that Trevor hadn't been paying his bills. It sounds like whoever took your bracelet was just trying to get even. That's why I think you should stop snooping around, stay some place other than your apartment until things blow over. At least until Trevor's killer is caught. And try to keep a low profile.''

"I have a business to run.''

"Hard to run dead.''

She got to her feet, put the gun on the coffee table and turned to him again. "I took the bullets out before I came out of the bedroom.''

"I know.'' He shrugged. "Otherwise, I would have taken the weapon away from you.''

He was an impossible man. She went back into the bathroom. Her bikini was still wet, but she closed the door and put it on, anyway. It helped cool her anger. "Where's my wet suit?''

"Just take the shirt,'' he called through the closed door. "It's an old one.''

She put the shirt back on. The cloth was worn

and soft and smelled a little like him. She'd get it back to him tomorrow.

When she came out, he was sitting where she'd left him, drinking his beer.

"Are you going to try to find out who killed Trevor?"

He shook his head. "I stay clear of ongoing murder investigations. It keeps me out of trouble."

She studied him for a long moment, feeling that electric excitement in the air between them. She didn't believe for a moment that if they made love again it would be anything but amazing. Maybe even more amazing than last night.

She ached for him to take her in his arms again, ached to feel his touch once more on her skin. But more than that, to feel that connection she'd felt between them. More than sex. Much more.

"About last night in the cottage—"

"Do me a favor," he said interrupting her. "Don't make me have to rescue you again. Tonight makes us even, okay?"

Even? She glared at him. "You're scared, aren't you."

He looked surprised.

"You're afraid of what would happen if we made love again." She couldn't believe the brazen words coming out of her mouth.

He couldn't seem to, either. He laughed and shook his head as he got up from his chair. She watched him go out onto the deck and pull her wet suit off the railing. He stayed there in the shadowy darkness, holding her wet suit out to her. "I think you better get going before I prove you wrong and disappoint us both. Let's just keep last night a memory, okay?''

She walked to him, snatched the wet suit from his fingers and crossed the deck to the opening in the railing. Once on the dock, she started the long walk to her van.

The dock felt warm under her bare feet as she left. A quiet darkness had settled over the marina. A light fog had moved in off the lake. The marina lights cast an eerie glow over the water.

She didn't look back at the houseboat until she reached the stand of pines where she'd left her van. Mackenzie Cooper was leaning against the boat railing, looking out into the darkness.

Just the sight of him made her ache. But Mackenzie Cooper had made it clear that last night was a mistake. One he didn't plan to repeat. Unfortunately it didn't make her want him any less.

What was it about last night and her that seemed to scare him? He didn't seem like a man who scared easily.

And she didn't believe for a moment that he wasn't looking for Trevor's killer. Which meant they'd be seeing each other again. Soon.

Chapter Ten

After a sleepless night watching Jill's apartment, Mac returned to the houseboat, took a cold shower and was getting dressed when his cell phone rang. He hoped it was Shane, who, Mac worried, was hiding, trying to figure out how to turn twelve gold coins into cash.

"Hello?" His hope was dashed at the sound of Pierce's voice.

"Well?" Pierce said.

"Well, what? You didn't really expect me to find your...merchandise this soon, did you?" Mac snapped back.

The silence on the other end of the line made it clear that Pierce had.

"I checked with my ranch foreman," Pierce said, sounding put out. "Shane did work on the ranch. For a week. He quit. So did his buddy who was hired with him, some guy who called himself Buffalo Boy."

Buffalo Boy. "I assume he has a real name," Mac said.

"Marvin. Marvin Dodd. You realize how important it is that the contents of that box don't just start turning up, don't you?''

Mac groaned to himself. ''I have another call coming in. I'll let you know as soon as I have something.'' He clicked off. What a pompous ass, he thought, as he took the other call.

''Mackenzie? It's Charley Johnson.'' Charles was one of the few people on earth Mac let call him Mackenzie.

The tone of his cop friend's voice scared him. Had Shane been found?

''I just got a report on that ring you called me about,'' Charley said. ''You're right. It was stolen. Are you sitting down?''

He wasn't.

''A seventeen-year-old girl by the name of Tara French was wearing that ring the night she disappeared from Bigfork seven years ago,'' Charley said. ''The ring had belonged to her grandmother. It was made especially for her, so it's very distinctive—and valuable. Mackenzie, Tara French was one of eleven young women who've disappeared in that area over the past twenty years. Where the hell did you get this ring?''

Mac dropped into a chair, all the ramifications knocking the wind out of him. ''I've got a human skull that might go with it. But I need this kept under wraps until we're sure. If I get the skull to you—''

Charley let out a curse. ''We can't sit on this with a serial killer out there running loose and you with important evidence.''

''If I'm right, the killer is dead, Charley,'' Mac

said. "Just give me forty-eight hours. I'll get the skull to you this morning. How long do you think it will take for an ID?"

Silence. "It will probably take me that long to get dental records on the eleven victims. Damn, I hope you're right about the killer being dead."

When Mac hung up, he thought about Jill and how she would take the news, if he was right about Trevor. Trevor had given her a ring that had belonged to a girl who'd been missing for seven years.

Mac uttered a vicious curse. To think that Jill had been engaged to a serial killer! Was it possible the other bodies were buried out there? Is that why Trevor had been "developing" Inspiration Island?

So what had he been doing out there? Reburying the bodies? Or moving them? But moving them where?

To the south end of the island, Mac thought with a start. To the swampy part where the mud was like quicksand.

The cell phone rang again, making him jump. "Hello?"

"I heard you were looking for a guy named Shane?" a young male voice asked.

Mac's pulse took off. "Yes, I am."

"You a cop?"

"No. A relative." Sometimes that was worse.

"He was living at Curtis Lakeview Apartments with a bunch of guys. Unit number seven. Does that help?"

"Thanks. I'll leave something for you at the Beach Bar. Just tell the bartender you're a friend of mine.'' He hung up. Curtis Lakeview Apartments. He felt as if the clock was ticking faster as he got into his pickup and drove north.

Curtis Lakeview Apartments had no view of the lake. Had no view at all. It was seven units stuck back in the pines, hastily thrown up and now quickly coming down.

The place was dead quiet. Either everyone was still asleep at this time of the morning, or some actually had jobs. Mac guessed that more than likely most of the units were empty. The building looked as if it could be condemned at any moment.

He wasn't expecting to find Shane here. By now Shane would have heard about Trevor Forester's murder. His nephew might not have the good sense to skip town, but he would be smart enough to change his address.

At least Mac hoped so. If Pierce was right about the collection being more valuable as a set than split up, then Trevor would have been trying to find a buyer. It made sense, given what he'd heard about Trevor Forester—that Trevor needed money and would even steal for it. Trevor must have been planning to skip town for some time now.

But now he was dead, and Mac feared Shane had the coins. It was how the kid had come to have the coins that worried him, since someone else was frantically looking for them. The shadowy figure on the videotape?

Mac groaned, wondering what plan Shane had to sell the coins. Shane wouldn't have the contacts or the patience to try to sell the coins as a set. He would try to dump the coins quickly, any way he could, and he'd leave a trail the other thief could follow. Shane was going to get himself killed, sure as hell.

The only hope Mac had of saving his nephew was to find him before he got rid of the coins.

Mac tried the door to the apartment. It was locked. He pulled out a credit card, inserted it between the door and jamb, and heard the click as the lock opened. Cautiously, he turned the knob. The door swung inward.

It was a studio apartment with only two pieces of furniture: a lawn chair and a card table.

It appeared his nephew had left in a hurry. There were stinky fast-food containers on the table, the chair was overturned and dirty clothing lay on the floor, along with a couple of magazines and newspapers and some junk mail.

Shane was definitely not getting his cleaning deposit back.

One small pale-green square of paper on the floor caught Mac's eye. He stooped to pick it up. It was a paycheck stub with Shane's name on it and Inspiration Island Enterprises. Made sense. Shane had worked for Trevor Forester on the island.

Mac pocketed the stub and checked his watch. He had a funeral to go to. Maybe he'd get lucky. Maybe Shane would show up at Trevor's funeral. It was something the kid was dumb enough to do.

DRESSED IN A PLAIN black dress and a hat with a veil that had belonged to her mother, Jill slipped quietly into the back of the church at Trevor's funeral. She didn't want her presence to upset Heddy.

Alistair was right. Heddy had opened the service to the entire town. The church was packed. Jill didn't have to worry about being seen.

From behind the veil, she looked for the other Scarlett and Mackenzie Cooper. Jill wasn't sure how much of what he'd told her the previous night she could believe. One thing she was sure of: there was a lot more going on with him—and Trevor's murder.

Heddy had insinuated that the murder of her son was somehow related to the other Scarlett. Jill knew she wouldn't feel safe until Trevor's murderer was caught. Maybe Mac was right. Maybe these attacks on her had to do with Trevor's misdeeds. But she suspected it was more complicated than that. She had a feeling that Mackenzie Cooper knew what was going on, and that was why he'd tried to warn her off.

If the other Scarlett was the same woman Trevor had supposedly been going to marry and run away with, then the woman would be here at the funeral, if for no other reason than to spit on his grave—assuming she'd found out that Trevor had cashed in her plane ticket.

Or maybe the woman had really loved Trevor and was here sobbing her eyes out. Uh-huh. Or maybe she'd just been after the Forester money to start with.

In any case, there was no way Jill was going to find her here. Too many people. And too quiet. Jill's only hope was to recognize the woman's voice.

She spotted her father and Zoe in the crowd and dozens of other people she knew. But she didn't see Mac.

Jill half listened to the service, thinking about Trevor. He had only dated her to please his father—and for the money. She almost felt sorry for him. Almost. What bothered her most was her own culpability. She'd wanted to believe Trevor. She'd been so busy going to college, getting her business going, making it successful, that she hadn't had time for romance—but her heart must have yearned for it more than she'd known, a discovery she'd made that night in the lake cottage with Mackenzie Cooper. As she stood at the back of the church, she didn't see him, but that didn't mean he wasn't here.

Maybe he'd been telling the truth. Maybe he couldn't care less who killed Trevor. Just like he couldn't care less about her? Or ever making love with her again?

The service, thankfully, was short, since the day was already hot even this early in the morning. She followed all the other cars out to the cemetery. By the time she reached the burial site, cars lined both sides of the narrow cemetery roads. She knew the cemetery well, because she came here weekly to put flowers on her mother's grave, so she parked the bakery delivery van well away from all the other cars and cut across to where the crowd was already twelve deep and others were coming in behind her.

She searched from behind her veil for the other Scarlett, a foolish endeavor since she had no idea what the woman looked like. She sensed someone moving through the crowd toward her and turned to see Arnie. He stood next to her.

"I wanted to apologize," he said quietly without looking at her. "That was really stupid what I did last night."

Yes, she thought, it was. "Let's just forget about it. Just like the night in the cottage," she whispered back.

He glanced at her as if surprised. Had he thought he'd blown it by kissing her? He had, of course, but she'd decided to keep it from him until she found out why he'd lied.

She felt a chill at the notion that the killer could be any of the people surrounding the grave—or standing next to her. Her gaze stopped on one man standing off by a tree a few yards away. Mackenzie Cooper. He'd been watching her, and he didn't look the least bit happy to see Arnie with her. That cheered her.

When her gaze met Mac's, her heart took off like a speedboat. She felt a small thrill and knew he'd felt it, too, as she watched him drag his gaze away first. He seemed to be looking for someone in the crowd.

She looked around, as well. When she couldn't help herself and glanced in his direction again, Mac was gone. But she felt some satisfaction in the fact that he'd attended the funeral. She was more certain than before that he was investigating Trevor's murder. What she didn't understand was why. Unless he felt bad that he hadn't been able to save Trevor.

The pastor finished speaking. Jill caught sight of

Heddy through a break in the crowd. She was crying, hanging on to Alistair for support. It was a sight Jill would never forget, the two of them standing beside their only son's grave, both devastated.

With the service over, a murmur of voices moved like a wave through the crowd. One voice carried on the morning air. Jill jerked around as she tried to locate the woman she'd heard speaking behind her. She'd know that voice anywhere. The other Scarlett.

Jill could catch only snatches of the woman's voice.

"Trevor...blame...awful."

Nor could she see the woman's face, only the woman's hat, as the voice moved away from the gravesite and along the row of parked cars.

Jill followed the hat, a floppy black disk of a hat with a red rose on the crown, and the strident voice.

"Heartless...cold...bitch."

Jill wondered who the woman was talking about. The black hat stopped beside one of the cars, then moved toward the other side of the cemetery. Jill spotted the red Saturn parked behind a stand of trees at the far side. The woman had the nerve to drive Jill's car to the funeral!

Jill tried to move through the dispersing crowd of people and cars, but saw that it was going to be impossible to reach the woman before she drove off.

Determined not to let the other Scarlett get away, Jill cut back across the cemetery, hurrying for her van, knowing she'd never be able to catch the woman on foot.

As Jill started the engine of The Best Buns in

Town van, the other Scarlett looked back, saw her and rushed to the Saturn. A moment later the Saturn roared toward one of the less-used exits away from the line of cars leaving the cemetery.

Jill raced after the other Scarlett, taking several of the service roads, all the time keeping the red Saturn in sight through the trees and gravestones.

She couldn't let the woman get away. Not this time, she thought, remembering two nights ago at Trevor's condo when the person driving the car had struck her in the head and taken off.

Jill was dying to know what the woman had been doing in Trevor's condo, what she'd been looking for in the bedroom and if she'd found it.

The red Saturn sped toward the exit, traveling at a right angle to Jill's van. Jill floored the van as she raced down the narrow cemetery road that with luck would connect with the road the other Scarlett was on—before the woman got there.

Jill reached the road, hit the brakes and skidded to a stop in the middle—blocking the exit with the van just seconds before the Saturn got there. Jill braced herself, half expecting the other Scarlett to broadside her.

The woman seemed to consider that option. But at the last minute, hit the brakes, bringing the Saturn to a dust-boiling stop in the middle of the road.

Jill leaped from the van and jerked the Saturn's door open before the other Scarlett had a chance to shift into reverse. Jill grabbed the car keys from the ignition, killing the engine.

"What are you doing?"

"This is my car!" Jill yelled. "Get out."

The woman had taken off her black hat, and Jill noted that the length of their hair was their only resemblance to one another. The woman's hair was a dingy brown and straight as string. Her nose was too big for her face. So was her mouth and her voice—

"Trevor gave me this car."

"He borrowed it from me," Jill snapped. "Check the registration and title."

"He *paid* for it," the woman shot back defiantly.

"He did not!" Jill wanted to drag the woman bodily from the car, but she restrained herself. "He didn't even pay for your airline ticket himself." The woman's surprised reaction confirmed what Jill suspected. "You're Rachel, aren't you. Were you looking for your ticket night before last in his bedroom? I suppose by now you know that he cashed it in."

Once again, the woman's expression confirmed it. "He did it because of you! He told me that you said you'd rather see him dead than with me."

"I didn't even know you existed," Jill said. "Haven't you figured out by now that Trevor lied to us both?"

"None of that matters," Rachel said, looking around nervously as if afraid someone might be listening. But the other mourners were too far away to hear. "Please, just leave me alone. If someone sees us together—"

"Who would care if they saw us together?" Jill asked, remembering that Heddy said she'd seen Scarlett O'Hara get off a boat at the dock a little after nine-thirty—just before Rachel had opened the cottage door. Rachel must have known about Trevor's meeting with Mac.

"That scene at the cottage was just a ruse to make it look as if you *thought* I was in there with Trevor, when all the time you knew better, didn't you?" Jill said in surprise. "You knew Trevor was dead."

"Stop asking questions about Trevor's murder, or you'll wish you had," Rachel spat.

The woman's words startled Jill. "I couldn't care less about you or who killed Trevor. I just want my car—and you to tell the sheriff you saw me in the cottage that night. Unless there's a reason you don't want to come forward?" The same reason she was far back in the crowd at the funeral hiding under a large black hat. Unless…she not only knew that Trevor was dead that night, she knew who did it— because she herself had put those two slugs in his heart.

The woman glanced around again. "Is that all you want? You can have the car. As for the sheriff—" she dug in her purse on the seat beside her and pulled out her cell phone "—I'll tell them right now. Then I want you to leave me alone. Trevor told me all about you," she said as she dialed 911. "He said you were a cold fish in bed and dangerous. I want nothing to do with you."

A cold fish, indeed. Jill felt her blood boil. It was all she could do not to drag the woman bodily from her car.

She looked down at the key ring in her hand. It was the one she'd given Trevor with her car key and her apartment key on it. Now there was only one key. So who had the old key to her apartment? The man in the black ski mask who'd gotten in the night before last?

"You're the one who sent that man over to take back the gifts Trevor had given me, aren't you."

"I don't know what you're talking about," Rachel said as she waited for the line to ring.

The emergency number should have answered by now, Jill thought. She started to reach for the phone when the woman said into the phone that she needed help. Her car was being hijacked by a crazy woman.

"Here, he wants to speak with you, Ice Princess," the other Scarlett said, holding out the cell phone.

Jill took it and said, "Hello, this is Jill Lawson and—"

In that instant Rachel gave Jill a shove away from the car and slammed the door, locking it. The engine roared to life a moment later, then the tires threw up gravel as the car lurched backward.

Jill jumped clear as Rachel tore up the road in reverse for a few dozen yards to a side road, turned and took off in a cloud of dust.

The woman apparently had a spare key, and she must have taken it from her purse when she'd gotten out the cell phone.

"She's stealing my car!" Jill yelled into the phone before realizing there was no one on the other end of the line. The other Scarlett hadn't called 911.

Jill scrambled to the van, backed it up and turned down the road, hoping to catch up with the Saturn and Rachel. But by the time she reached the cemetery exit, the woman was gone.

Braking hard, Jill slammed her fist down on the steering wheel, then picked up Rachel's cell phone and dialed 911.

"We've already got an all points bulletin out for the car and driver," Deputy Duncan told her after she explained what had happened. "Give me her cell-phone number."

She did and Duncan said, "That's Trevor's cell phone."

"He always had it with him," Jill told the deputy. "How did she get it?"

"Well, she doesn't have it anymore," he said quietly. "You do."

Jill hung up, angry and frustrated. Who knew how long it would take the sheriff's department to find the Saturn and the other woman? And now she had Trevor's cell phone and only her word that she'd taken if from the other Scarlett.

She looked up to see Mackenzie Cooper's pickup in the line of funeral cars leaving the cemetery. Like the rest of Bigfork, he'd witnessed her confrontation with the other Scarlett from a distance—just too great a distance to prove anything.

As she shifted the van into gear, she watched his pickup head down the lake road and wondered again why he had come to the funeral of a man he'd never met.

IN HIS REARVIEW mirror, Mac saw The Best Buns in Town van tailing him. He took a quick right, a left, then another right. When he looked back again, the van was still there. He couldn't outrun her in the pickup, not with the camper on the back.

He cursed and pulled over to the curb, waiting until she pulled in behind him before getting out and walking back to the van.

She rolled down her window.

"What the hell do you think you're doing?" he asked.

"Following you." She had the same determined set to her jaw that he'd seen last night. No gun, though, which was a plus. "You lied."

He stared at her. "What?"

"You felt something the other night."

"Is that what this is about?" Her look dared him to lie again. "All right, I felt something. Happy?"

"Something amazing. Something more than great sex."

He smiled in spite of himself. "Something amazing. Something more than great sex. Okay? Now that we have that settled, don't follow me." He turned to walk away.

"I know where you can find Marvin Dodd," she said. "You are looking for him, right?" she said when he was standing at her driver's-side window again.

That was the trouble with a small town like Bigfork. But he knew his trouble ran much deeper. "Just because it felt like more than great sex the other night—"

"This has nothing to do with that," she said.

He gave her a give-me-a-break look.

"Do you want to find Marvin or not?"

He waited for her to ask him why he was looking for Marvin, but she didn't. "What's the catch?"

"No catch. Marvin worked for Trevor on the island. That's why you're looking for him. You're trying to find Trevor's murderer."

It was news to him that Marvin had also worked for Trevor, but he shouldn't have been surprised. She looked so pleased with herself he hated to bust her bubble.

"Wrong. I'm looking for my nephew."

"Whatever," she said. "I guess I'll just have to find Trevor's killer on my own." Her brown eyes flashed, reminding him of another fire he'd seen burning in all that amber when he'd kissed her last night on his houseboat.

"Have a death wish, do you?"

"No, just the opposite. I guess because I was Trevor's fiancée—well one of them, anyway—I'm involved. Up to my neck, and I think you are, too. If you won't tell me what's going on, I'll just follow you and find out for myself. And I should warn you, I've had a really bad day so far."

He cursed under his breath and turned on his heel. "Get in the truck," he said over his shoulder.

She scrambled from the van, catching up with him at the pickup.

He didn't look at her as she climbed into the passenger side. Couldn't. He was too angry with her. "I'm trying to protect you."

"Well, stop," she said, looking out the windshield, waiting for him to start the engine.

What the hell was he going to do with her? "You are an incredibly stubborn woman."

"Thank you."

"That wasn't a compliment."

She smiled and looked over at him. "Why is it so hard for you to be honest with me?"

"You have heard of privileged information, haven't you? I'm on a case." He put the truck into gear.

"Trevor's dead," she said.

"It's another case." He could feel her gaze on him.

"Turn right up here and head down the lake toward Polson," she ordered.

"Why were you chasing that woman in the red Saturn?" he asked as he pressed the accelerator.

"That woman was the other Scarlett and she was driving *my* car!"

"Seems she's still driving your car."

She shot him a warning look. "You could have helped me."

"I didn't realize you needed help. Did you get her name?"

"No, I only know her first name—Rachel. She got away before I could get anything but mad," Jill said. "She's driving *my* car and she says Trevor gave it to her."

"He probably did." Mac watched her tug at her lower lip with her teeth. "I take it the two of you had words?" He was surprised to see tears in her eyes.

"She told me I was a cold fish, and that's why Trevor—"

"Bull," Mac snapped. "Trevor was a fool and obviously not much of a lover." He handed her his handkerchief. "Trevor was out of his league with a woman like you."

Jill looked over at him and smiled through her tears. "You can be pretty nice when you want to be."

He focused his attention on his driving, warning himself that being too nice to Jill was trouble. Too easily he could find her in his arms—and they both knew where that would lead.

"Turn up here on the right," she said, all business again. "Marvin lives in a trailer out on Finley Point." She smiled. "I grew up in Bigfork. News travels fast. Especially if you know who to ask."

"You've been asking questions about me?" He wasn't happy to hear this. "Who told you I was looking for Marvin?"

She smiled. "You're actually looking for a nineteen-year-old named Shane Ramsey. Marvin Dodd used to be his roommate. Well?"

"Nice work. You really are determined to get yourself killed, aren't you."

"I thought your investigation had nothing to do with Trevor's death."

"Did you ever think that just being around me might be dangerous?" he asked, shooting her a look.

Her smile broadened. "After the other night in the cottage, I know just how dangerous you can be."

He growled under his breath and tried to change

the subject. "So you've lived here your whole life?"

"You sound aghast at the thought. I'm content here. It's a great place to live."

"I don't doubt it." He remembered the last time he was content somewhere.

"I'm sure you've heard gossip about me around town," she said. "How bad is it? What's everyone saying? What a fool I was to think Trevor wanted to marry me?"

"Everything I heard about you was glowing," he said. "True, people wondered what you saw in Trevor... What *did* you see in him?"

She stared out at the passing green blur of pines for a long moment, so long he didn't think she was going to answer. "Trevor could be quite charming. I think he was an actor—he would play whatever role he thought you wanted." She shrugged. "And he paid attention to the small things." She looked away.

"Like what?" he asked, needing to know what she'd seen in the man. Now more than ever.

"I had this horrible experience when I was sixteen," she said. "I never hitchhiked, but this one night I was at a party and my ride's car broke down and I was frantic to get home on time, so I did something really stupid. I took off by myself, walking down the lake road. It was really late, one of those dark cloudy nights, and this car stopped for me."

Mac felt his chest constrict. Dear God.

"I never saw his face. It was just a voice in the darkness of the car. He asked if I needed a ride. I didn't even pay any attention to the car. It was just large and black and I started to get in. Then, I don't know why, I changed my mind. I guess somehow I…knew.'' She looked out her side window, away from him. He saw her chin quiver, and it was all he could do not to reach for her. "The driver grabbed my wrist, but I was wearing this bracelet my aunt had given me for my birthday. The bracelet saved me. It came off and I was able to pull free and run. I ran into the trees. He got out of the car and started to follow me, but must have changed his mind. I heard the car leave. I'd never been so scared in my life.''

Mac reached over and took the hand resting on her thigh. It was cold as ice. She was shaking. But so was he. "You must have been terrified." She nodded. "And you told Trevor about this?" He took his hand back to steer the pickup down the narrow, twisting road to Finley Point. In places, as it wound through cherry orchards and pines, the road was like a tunnel.

"The day after I told Trevor, he brought me a present," she said. "A silver charm bracelet with my name on it like the one I'd lost. Trevor said the bracelet had brought me luck once before—and would again." She looked over at Mac, tears in her eyes. "That's the kind of thing Trevor did." She rubbed her bare wrist.

Mac felt as if he'd been kicked in the chest as he thought about the charm bracelet Trevor had given her. The same one the burglar had taken the other night. A bracelet like the one she'd lost when she was sixteen? Or the exact same bracelet? If Mac was right about Trevor Forester...

He pulled over to the side of the road. He could see the lake stretching clear blue to a horizon, broken only by a single white sail in the distance. "There's something I have to tell you."

He'd been worried before, but now he was terrified for her. He told himself that Trevor was dead. Jill was safe. But her apartment had been burglarized. Worse, the burglar had attacked her, taken the bracelet—and asked about the engagement ring.

Mac couldn't pretend it had been someone Trevor owed money to. Not anymore. Nor could he keep the truth from Jill anymore.

"My nephew was involved in a robbery—with Trevor Forester," Mac said. "They stole some coins. Trevor's now dead and the coins are missing. But there's more." He looked into her eyes. Deep and brown. The flecks of gold shimmering in the summer sunlight.

"I picked up your engagement ring that night in the cottage, along with your panties. The ring appeared to have been old and the inscription filed down. I called a friend of mine who's a cop in Kalispell. I had a feeling that the job Trevor pulled off with my nephew probably wasn't his first."

"You aren't telling me that the engagement ring Trevor gave me was stolen?"

"Jill, the ring belonged to a teenaged girl who disappeared from Bigfork seven years ago," Mac said. "She was never found."

Chapter Eleven

Jill felt the blood drain from her head. "No." She remembered the stories in the papers over the years. Teenaged girls who'd come to the area to work for the summer just disappearing without a trace.

"I sent the skull I found on the island to Kalispell this morning," Mac said, his voice sounding far away. "I know I told you it was probably an old gravesite, but I'm afraid that skull hasn't been in the ground very long."

Jill shook her head, feeling the sting of tears in her eyes. "You think Trevor…"

"I think whoever killed those girls kept a piece of their jewelry as a souvenir," Mac said softly. "I also think there is a good possibility that the killer buried the girls on the island."

A chill quaked through her as she recalled the skull she'd seen in Mac's duffel bag. "Tell me Trevor couldn't do something so horrible." But she thought of how he'd lied and stolen and cheated. How he'd planned to leave the country.

"He gave you the ring," Mac said.

Yes, he'd given her the ring. The ring he'd said

was an old family heirloom. A lie. But could it really have been Trevor Forester in the car that stopped for her on the lake road that night fourteen years ago? She'd been sixteen. Trevor would have been twenty. Old-sounding to a sixteen-year-old.

She closed her eyes, remembering the headlights as the car came up the road and stopped. She squeezed her eyes shut more tightly, trying to remember, to see into the darkness inside the car. A large, dark car. His father's car? The whir of the electric window on the passenger side coming down. A voice from the blackness inside as she leaned down and took hold of the door handle, thinking only about getting home on time.

Her eyes flew open, the taste of fear in her mouth, the sound of her heart hammering in her ears as he grabbed her wrist, and then her pulling free, running, running for her life.

She warned herself not to cry. The last thing Mac needed was a bawling woman on his hands. Actually, he didn't seem to need any woman at all, especially her.

He handed her a tissue from the glove box.

She didn't cry. She balled up the tissue in her hand. She wasn't a sixteen-year-old girl anymore. No, she was a strong, independent woman. And the past few days had only made her stronger, more resilient, definitely more outspoken—almost brazen and, surprisingly, less afraid of her feelings. "It could have been him."

"I know. That's what scares me." His words sent a shaft of heat through her.

She looked at him and their eyes locked.

After Trevor, she knew she should have been gun-shy when it came to men. But Mackenzie Cooper was a different breed of male. She was intimately aware of that, she thought as she gazed into the deep blue of his eyes. He hadn't forgotten the other night in the cottage any more than she had.

He reached for her, cupped the nape of her neck just as he'd done last night on the boat and pulled her toward him as if he needed to feel her in his arms as badly as she needed to be there. "This is just lust," he whispered against her hair.

"Mmm-hmm."

"We'd both regret it if we make love again."

"Mmm."

He kissed her hair, her temple, her cheek, angling toward her mouth. Her breath caught in her throat as his lips hovered over hers. In his eyes, she saw the fear. Did he really believe they would be disappointed, regretful? She didn't think so.

His mouth lowered slowly, painfully to hers. He brushed a kiss over her lips. She sighed and leaned into him. His body was warm and hard. He groaned against her mouth. Her lips parted and his mouth met hers fully. The kiss deepened. The tip of his tongue slid slowly across her upper lip, and she thought she would die with wanting him.

"Oh, Jill," he said with a sigh as he pulled back to look at her, cupping her face in his hands.

What was he so afraid of?

His gaze moved over her face like a caress, then he pulled away, groaning. As he leaned back in his seat, he ran a hand over his face, then gripped the steering wheel with both hands as he looked out the windshield—not at her.

Disappointment made her eyes well up with tears. She felt weak, the ache in her crying out for him. She wanted to touch his broad shoulders, feel the warmth of his shirt. To lean her face into his chest and breathe in the clean, masculine scent of him.

"I'm sorry." He cleared his throat. "Where did Trevor say he got the engagement ring?"

She sat back, her heart pounding, the ache inside making her want desperately to cry. She took a breath. Let it out.

He looked at her. His look was a plea. *Just tell me about the ring.*

She took another breath and said, "Trevor told me the ring belonged to his favorite great-aunt, but I remember Heddy's surprise when she first saw the ring." Jill's voice didn't betray the unbearable need inside her. "I thought it was because Heddy didn't think he should have given me such a valuable family heirloom."

"He obviously lied about where he'd gotten the ring," Mac said, "and his mother covered for him."

"Yes, that would be like Heddy." Jill couldn't bear to look at Mac. She glanced out at the lake and remembered something. "The day he found out the island was for sale, Trevor was beside himself. We were at his parents' house and he was practically begging his father to buy the island for him. I remember him saying, 'If I don't develop it, someone else will.'" She shivered. "Alistair said he'd never seen his son so excited or anxious. At the time we all thought Trevor wanted to prove himself to his father, and Inspiration Island was going to be the means.'' She looked over at Mac now. ''But Trevor's had the island for months. I would think if his purpose was to move the bodies, he would have done it by now.''

''I suspect he'd forgotten where all the bodies were buried. Plus, animals have gotten into the remains. I suspect he was moving the bodies to the south end of the island, thinking he could hide them behind the restricted area. Or maybe that was where he'd buried them to start with and was just reburying them. I think the bodies were floating up in the mud. The skull I found was sticking up out of some weeds.''

She thought she might throw up. ''We have to tell the sheriff.''

''I asked my cop friend for forty-eight hours,'' Mac said. ''It will take that long to try to get an ID on the skull through dental records. Give me the same amount of time. Let me find my nephew. We still don't know who killed Trevor. Or why. And my client's coins are still missing. I'm afraid any one of those factors could get Shane killed if the authorities became involved.''

''You can't tell me who your client is?''

''Sorry. He's a victim of Trevor Forester, too. Just like us, it seems,'' Mac said, meeting her gaze. ''I still don't know why Trevor sent me a Rhett Butler costume and told me to meet him in the lake cottage. That concerns me.''

"Yes." She had to agree. "I also wish I knew what Trevor had planned for *me* the night of the party." When she thought of what the man might have been capable of...

"Can you hold off going to the sheriff for forty-eight hours?" Mac asked.

"Maybe we can make a deal."

He groaned.

"I help you find your nephew and you help me find the other Scarlett. What do you say?" He started to argue, but she stopped him. "Please, don't try to warn me about the dangers, okay?" She gently touched her bruised forehead, remembering the man in the black ski mask.

Mac sighed, then nodded with obvious reluctance.

She gave him a smile, as much as it hurt. "Marvin lives just up the road."

"WAIT HERE," Mac said as he pulled up in front of the blue-and-white striped trailer Marvin rented. Jill didn't argue about staying in the pickup as he climbed out.

He wore jeans, a pale-blue cotton shirt and a dark suede jacket, his idea of funeral attire. Under his jacket, the weapon in his shoulder holster fit snugly against his ribs, not that he expected he would have to use it. At least he hoped not.

He could feel Jill watching him as he knocked on the side of the trailer and then tried the door.

Unlocked. Almost like an invitation. He opened the door and stepped in, drawing the weapon from the shoulder holster. The place looked and smelled like a summer-kid rental. It was cluttered with clothes, the counters covered in beer bottles and empty fast-food boxes, and the air smelled of stale beer and pepperoni pizza.

He found Marvin passed out in a back bedroom of the trailer. He appeared to be the only one home this late morning. Either he didn't have to go to work yet or he didn't have a job. Likely the latter. Mac called his name. Loudly.

Marvin squinted up from the crumpled covers of the twin bed stuffed in a corner of the otherwise packed-with-junk bedroom.

"Who the hell are you?" Marvin looked about fifteen, but according to the driver's license Mac took from the wallet lying on the bedside table, the kid was nineteen—the same age as Shane. His greasy brown hair hung in strings about his acne-covered face, and he looked as if he had the hangover from hell, but there was no doubt he was the kid who'd been driving the getaway van the night of the coin theft at Pierce's.

Mac grimaced just looking at him. "Get up."

"If this is about the rent, you gotta talk to my roommate," the kid said, and covered his head with the blanket.

"It's about the robbery. The one you pulled off with Trevor Forester." Mac opened the back door, needing a little fresh air.

Marvin's head came out from under the covers. "I don't know what you're talking out."

"Sure you do. Get dressed." He turned and saw Jill standing in the trailer's kitchen. He started down the hall toward her, angry. Damn, why couldn't she just run her bakery and let him do his job?

"What do you think you're—" The rest of the words were cut off by the look on her face. She was holding a paper bag in one hand and a bakery roll in the other, her eyes large, her face white as snow.

She held the roll out to him.

He stared down at the perfect impression of a double-eagle, twenty-dollar gold piece in the baked dough. "Where did you find this?"

She pointed to the trash.

That was when he noticed the bag in her hand and the name on it: The Best Buns In Town.

Just then he heard Marvin go out the back door of the trailer.

Mac swore and went after him. He caught the punk kid a few yards from the trailer and took him down with a football tackle that knocked the wind out of them both.

He jerked Marvin to his feet and dragged him back toward the trailer. "Are you a cop or something?" the skinny kid whined.

Mac pushed Marvin in through the front door of the trailer and pointed to the kitchen table. "Sit."

He looked at Jill. She was right. She was up to her neck in this. He took the roll from her and showed Marvin the impression of a coin that had been baked in the dough. "Where are the coins?"

"I swear I don't know." He was dressed in thongs sandals, basketball shorts and a once-white T-shirt that hung on his scrawny frame.

"I know you were driving the van the night of

the robbery," Mac said to Marvin. "It's all on vid-eotape."

"Mr. Forester, Trevor, he said he needed some help. This guy owed him money and wouldn't pay, so we helped him. But I got the impression it had something to do with a woman."

Didn't it always? Mac shoved the roll with the coin impression in front of the kid's face. "The coins?"

Marvin swallowed, eyes wide. "My roommate is the one who had them, and he's gone."

"Who's your roommate?"

"Just some guy I worked with. He called himself Spider. That's all I know."

Mac heard Jill gasp. He shot her a look. Damn, it appeared she knew this Spider. "How exactly did your roommate end up with the coins?"

"I don't know. Really. He gave me one of the rolls, all right. The coin was baked inside it. It was my payment for the job."

This Spider had paid Marvin with one of the coins.

"Tell me you still have the coin."

Marvin seemed to hesitate, but only for a second. He hurried to a closet and dug around in the back, pulled out an old boot and upended it. A gold coin fell out and clinked on the worn linoleum floor.

Mac picked it up. It still had dough on it. "Did Spider kill Trevor for these?"

"I don't know anything about that, I swear. I didn't ask him. I wanted nothing to do with it. I just worked for Mr. Forester, okay?"

"And felony burglary was part of the job?"

"He offered me five hundred bucks to drive a van one night. It was a hell of a lot better than digging up bones on the island."

Mac shot Jill a look. Her skin had paled even more.

"Who was the other guy involved in the burglary?"

"Mr. Forester and Spider. That's all."

"You didn't see anyone else in the house?" Mac asked, remembering the shadow he'd seen on the video.

"I just drove the van, man."

That meant the fourth man was either already inside the house or had met them after they got out of the van. That man must have known about the surveillance cameras or just lucked out and stayed out of the picture. Except for his shadow.

"One more question. Who is Buffalo Boy?"

Marvin reddened. "It's just this name I picked up."

Mac nodded. "And you met Spider in Whitefish, right?"

Buffalo Boy nodded.

"You need to clean this place up, Marvin."

"No, man, somebody trashed it yesterday," the kid said. "At least they didn't take my stereo or anything."

"Let me guess—Spider hadn't dropped off your share yet?" Mac asked, holding up the half roll.

Marvin paled. "You think they were looking for the coins?"

Mac felt protective, probably because Marvin reminded him of Shane. ''You might consider lying low for a while.''

Taking the roll and the coin, he and Jill returned to the pickup. Some of the color had come back into her face. ''Any idea how that coin ended up inside the baked roll?'' he asked her after they were in the truck and pulling away.

''I'm afraid so,'' she said.

''And Spider? You know him?''

''I know just the person to ask about him,'' Jill said, sounding awful. ''My baking assistant, Zoe.''

JILL COULDN'T believe it. But then again, she could. Zoe was head over heels for this Spider guy. She was young and had an excuse for being naive and falling for a man's line.

But Jill was almost thirty, and look how she'd been conned by Trevor, a man who was a liar, a thief and maybe even a killer.

''The coins were baked into the rolls,'' she said, and realized Mac had figured that much out on his own.

Jill thought back to the morning of the party. Zoe had been excited because her boyfriend was going to stop by the bakery. Jill's father had called, saying he wouldn't be by because he had the flu, doubted he'd be going to the party, either, sorry. She'd left Zoe with the unbaked rolls while she'd run to the drugstore to get her father a few things.

''I let Zoe finish up the rolls the morning of the party. I should have known something was up, but she's been so anxious to learn and do things on her own... And her boyfriend was stopping by..."

"Spider, right?"

Jill nodded.

"The morning of the party?" Mac said, sounding surprised. "That means Spider had the coins *before* Trevor was killed. Where do we find this baking assistant of yours?"

"Summer school. Algebra II. Head back toward Bigfork."

"Let's hope they still have the coins," Mac said.

Jill was worried about Zoe. She'd trusted the girl. And now all she could think about was Zoe's reaction when she heard about Trevor's murder. How deep was the girl in all this?

AS THE SMALL summer-school class let out, the students and teacher left quickly. Jill stepped into the classroom and watched Zoe finish an algebra problem, then fold several papers and stuff them into her algebra book before she rose to her feet. Her hair was blue today like everything she wore, including her fingernail polish.

When she saw Jill, Zoe froze, fear in her eyes. She clutched her algebra book to her chest and looked from Jill to Mac and back again.

"We need to talk to you," Jill said. "This is Mackenzie Cooper. He's a private investigator looking for the coins you hid in the rolls you baked the morning of the party."

Zoe's face crumpled as she dropped back into the seat at her desk. Mac closed the classroom door.

"I had to help Spider!" Zoe cried. "He would have killed him if he found out."

"Who would have killed him?" Mac asked.

"Trevor," the girl said, close to tears.

"Is this Spider?" Mac asked as he walked over to her, opened his wallet and showed her a photo of a young man with blond hair, blue eyes and an angular face.

"Yes, that's him." Zoe looked up in confusion.

"His name is Shane Ramsey," Mac said. "He's my nephew and I have to find him. His life is in danger because of the coins, the ones you put into the rolls."

"I don't know where he is," she wailed. "He swears he didn't know Trevor was going to rob anyone that night."

"You'd think he'd get suspicious when Trevor told him to put on the ski mask," Mac said.

"I know it looks bad..." Zoe's eyes teared up.

Jill shot Mac a pleading look.

"He was afraid of Trevor," the girl said. "He didn't say it, but I knew. Trevor had hired him to do some work on the island."

"Do you know what work precisely?" Mac asked.

Zoe shook her head, then frowned. "One night though, when he picked me up, he said he'd been digging in muck all day and that he was going to quit, but the next time I saw him, he said Trevor wasn't going to let him quit. I got the impression that maybe Trevor had threatened him, you know?"

Digging in muck. "Yeah, I can see where Trevor

might have changed Spider's mind.'' Was that how Shane had gotten involved in the robbery? Had Trevor forced him? Or had Shane gone along willingly?

''Where are the coins now?''

Zoe shook her head. ''I don't know. Honestly.''

''How is it Spider ended up with them?'' Mac persisted.

Zoe hesitated. ''Trevor changed his mind. Said it was a big mistake taking the coins and that Spider had to return them. Trevor was acting all weird— like the guy they stole the coins from was going to kill him. There was no way Spider was going back there with those coins.''

Mac groaned. ''So my nephew decided to sell the coins, instead?''

''No,'' Zoe said indignantly. ''He had to come up with some way to return them without actually going there, you know?''

Jill nodded. ''So he hid the coins in the dough, then you baked them.''

''Spider called, left a message that the rolls were on their way and to look inside them,'' Zoe said.

''Not a bad idea. When were they delivered?'' Mac asked.

''The day of the party.''

Jill shot a look at Mac. The coins had been returned? Then why was Mac still looking for them?

''How many did Shane return?'' he asked.

Zoe smiled. ''You know, I kinda like the name Shane.''

"How many coins did he return?" Jill prodded her.

The girl blinked. "Oh, we returned all but two. Shane gave one to...someone because he thought that was only fair that he be paid—" Marvin, Jill surmised "—and he kept one. So I guess we sent ten rolls in the delivery."

"Tell me you didn't send the rolls in one of The Best Buns in Town bags," Jill said, almost adding, *like you did the one for Marvin.*

"Of course not," Zoe said. "We used a plain white bag. We didn't want him knowing where the rolls came from."

Thank goodness for that. Jill looked at Mac. "Where were these rolls delivered?" She figured to the home of the man Mac was working for.

"To Inspiration Island," Zoe said, making them both stare at her. Zoe nodded. "When Shane called back a second time to see if the guy got the first message, he said to deliver them to the island and leave them at some cove."

"Shane took them out by boat?"

Zoe shook her head. "He hired some kids to take them out. You know, just in case it was a trap."

Mac groaned. "How do you know the kids actually took the rolls to the island like they were told to?"

"Shane called him back the next morning. He got the rolls."

"But?" Jill said, hearing the *but* in Zoe's voice.

"But he wants the rest," she said, and sighed.

"The coins are part of a twelve-piece set," Mac

said. "I imagine the owner wants all twelve back. Shane never told you the man's name?"

She shook her head. "Shane's in trouble, isn't he."

"That's putting it mildly," Mac said. "There's a killer out there who seems willing to do anything to get these coins. You have to tell me where I can find Shane."

"I don't know, honest. He can't stay in one place. So he calls me at night from a pay phone."

"When he calls, I want you to talk him into calling me." Mac handed her his card. "If you care anything about him—"

"I love him." Zoe began to cry in earnest. "Please help him."

Jill put her arm around Zoe and looked beseechingly at Mac, who groaned.

Chapter Twelve

After Jill assured a teary-eyed Zoe that she wasn't going to fire her, Zoe promised to go home and stay there.

"What do we do now?" Jill asked Mac once they were back in his pickup.

"I wait to hear from Shane." And try to keep his distance from Jill. Her baking assistant had been a real surprise. He couldn't see anyone as straitlaced as Jill hiring a girl who looked like Zoe. And yet Jill had. He liked this woman more all the time—which wasn't the plan.

He glanced over at her. There were so many layers to this woman he knew he'd never see them all in a lifetime.

"While we wait, we find Rachel and complete our deal," he said. The sooner Jill went back to baking the better.

"And how do you propose we do that?"

"I'm a trained professional, remember? We consider where Trevor could have met her. I take it he spent a lot of time on the island, right? She probably doesn't live in his condo complex." Jill nodded. "So what does that leave?"

"Meals."

He smiled. "Oh, you're good." He had a pretty complete picture of Trevor Forester from everything he'd learned. "I doubt he spent much time in the kitchen cooking for himself, right?" Or much time alone. Nor did he probably have much trouble picking up women.

"Trevor? He couldn't boil water. And I didn't see much of him so..."

"Where did he eat?"

She thought about that for a moment. "I know of a couple of places."

The first one, a sandwich shop along the highway south of Bigfork, was a bust. No Rachel worked there or hung out there. They tried several fast-food places near Trevor's condo and finally stopped at a burger joint along the lake that also served alcohol.

"I don't know about you, but I'm hungry," Mac said, grinning as he pointed to one of the Employee of the Month photos on the wall.

"That's her!" Jill whispered. Rachel Wells, the name under the photo read. January's Employee of the Month. "I'm starved!"

Mac led them to a booth by the window so they could catch the last of the sunset—and keep an eye out for Rachel. He sat across from Jill and flipped open the plastic-covered menu, trying to concentrate on food rather than the woman across from him. "How does a cheeseburger deluxe sound to you?"

"Wonderful," she said, and seemed to relax.

But Rachel Wells, it appeared, wasn't working today. At least they didn't see her.

They talked about lakes and what they loved about them and how they couldn't imagine living away from water, then laughed that they had that in common, both pretty convinced they only had one thing in common and that was the night they'd shared in the cottage.

But Mac was learning just how much they shared. It made what happened between them the night in the cottage make more sense. He also noted that Jill was beautiful when she laughed. Her whole face lit up, her brown eyes dancing.

When the burgers arrived, Jill dug right in.

They had that in common, too, it seemed, he thought. They loved to eat. They ate in a comfortable, contented silence, appreciating their burgers and fries and each other. He felt as if he'd known this woman always. The closeness was almost painful for him.

When he'd finished eating, he pushed back his plate, sighed and looked at her. "That's the nicest meal I've had with a woman since…I can't remember when," he said as he watched her dunk the last of her fries in ketchup and take a bite.

She smiled and licked her lips. "What made it so nice? The fries? The burger?"

"You," he said truthfully.

She raised a brow. "Honesty becomes you. I feel comfortable with you, too. Maybe it's because of the other night in the cottage or maybe we would have felt this way, anyway."

"We'll never know," he said, and dug out his wallet to pay the check. What he did know was that they wouldn't be together now if it hadn't been for what happened in the cottage. He went out of his way to avoid attachments. He would have avoided Jill Lawson like the plague.

How could Trevor Forester not have seen what a kind, loving woman Jill was? Maybe Trevor wasn't looking for that kind of woman any more than he himself was, Mac thought.

She was watching him with her big doe eyes, studying him as if she could read his mind and found it amusing that he was fighting this spark— hell, forest fire—between them. How could she not see how hard he was struggling to keep his distance from her?

"It wouldn't work, you and me," he said, not sure who he was trying to convince. "I go wherever the wind blows me. You—"

"I own a bakery, an apartment, a building," she said, her gaze meeting his and holding it. "Definitely not compatible."

He knew she was making fun of him. And he couldn't blame her. What a fool he was, trying to convince her that their problem was location. Or that the air between them wasn't charged with current, or that he didn't want to take her in his arms and kiss her every time he looked at her, or that what they'd shared the other night wasn't incredible.

All powerful stuff. All wrong at this point in their lives. At any point in his. But damned if he didn't want to see where this chemistry took them—just as she did. Except…he knew exactly where it would take them. And he couldn't go there.

Jill had been hurt enough by Trevor Forester. Mac didn't want to cause her more pain. He knew that she'd be far more hurt if they became lovers again before he left. And he *would* leave.

The young blond waitress with the ponytail and bright red lipstick brought their bill. "Excuse me," Mac said. "I was hoping Rachel was working today. I promised a friend I'd tell her hello."

"Rachel?" The girl looked toward the kitchen and the cook. She lowered her voice. "I wouldn't mention Rachel if I were you. She hasn't shown up for work. Bud gave her the morning off for the funeral—Trevor Forester's funeral, you know. But she was supposed to work this afternoon."

Obviously Rachel hadn't been planning to give two weeks' notice before running off with Trevor. Or maybe she'd never planned to go because she'd planned to kill Trevor, instead.

"Are you a good friend of hers?" Jill asked.

The waitress made a so-so motion with her hand. "Rachel's all right. Not exactly friendly to other women, if you know what I mean. Prefers men."

Men? Plural? "I thought she and Trevor Forester were pretty serious," Jill said.

The waitress shrugged. "I never thought Trevor was serious about her. And it wasn't like Rachel didn't keep her options open—and so did Trevor." She bent down a little and whispered, "He asked me out just last week."

Jill found R. Wells in the phone directory in the

telephone booth outside the burger joint and read off the address to Mac. It was dark now. Still no call from Shane, and Mac was getting more worried all the time. He didn't think going over to Rachel's house was a good idea, but he knew Jill would go alone if they didn't.

"Why don't you call the sheriff's department and let them handle this?" he suggested.

"Come on, it doesn't appear they've made any effort to find her. I don't think they even believe she exists."

Mac couldn't argue that.

"I also don't want her to get away again," Jill said. "Arnie has a cousin who works next door to the sheriff's department. Arnie has known too much not to have been getting inside information. And if Trevor knew Rachel, then so did Arnie. Arnie was his shadow."

Rachel Wells lived in a small apartment north of Bigfork. Jill's red Saturn was nowhere to be seen.

"She doesn't know me. Why don't you let me go to the door? If she spots you, she might bolt."

"All right. Just don't let her get away."

He smiled. "I'll tackle her if she makes a run for it."

"You used to play football, didn't you?"

"A long time ago."

"I'll bet you were good. High school? College?"

"Both." This kind of talk was making him uncomfortable. He didn't tell anyone about his past. "Sit tight."

Mac knocked. No answer. He tried several more

times, then peered in the windows. The place looked as if it'd been ransacked. Impossible to tell if it had happened before or after Rachel Wells had packed up and cleared out. There was a photo on the floor, the frame and glass broken. It was the same woman as in the Employee of the Month photo.

He checked the back, then returned to the pickup and Jill. "It looks like she's taken off. The place has been ransacked."

Jill groaned. "I just know she's involved in Trevor's murder somehow. She warned me at the funeral that it was dangerous to be asking questions about the murder."

"I believe I told you the same thing," Mac said. "Call the sheriff's department. Maybe she left a clue in the apartment about where she went, and they can go in and find it."

He listened while Jill placed the call on her cell. Deputy Duncan wasn't in, so she left a message for him with Rachel Wells's name and address.

When she hung up she looked over at Mac. "Well, I guess that's it. I helped you find Marvin and you helped me find Rachel."

He looked out at the darkness, not wanting to leave her any more than he suspected she wanted him to. "Technically, we didn't find Rachel."

"True, and we might not," Jill said. "I'm sure she's skipped town. And to add insult to injury, probably in my car."

This was crazy. And dangerous. "I don't think you should be alone right now."

She shot him a look. "What are you suggesting?"

He had trouble saying the words. "I think I should stay with you, on your couch, at least for a while."

"I just got new locks—"

"Look," he said, turning to face her, "your couch has to be better than sleeping in the front of this truck every night."

She smiled at him. "You've been watching my apartment?"

"You didn't give me much choice," he said.

"Why?"

"So you wouldn't get killed."

"No," she said. "I mean why do you feel you have to protect me? What makes it your job?"

"After the other night…"

She started laughing. "Do you protect every woman you sleep with?"

"Of course not," he said, wishing he hadn't told her about the night vigils.

She raised a brow. "Then why me?"

"You know the answer to that. I made love with Trevor Forester's fiancée while he was being murdered just before he was going to hire me to find his killer."

She shook her head. "Nice try. But that isn't it."

He swore under his breath. "Are you going to let me stay on your couch or not?"

"Of course. I appreciate your wanting to protect me, although I don't think it's necessary."

"Let me be the judge of that." He started the truck and drove back to where they'd left her van earlier. "I'll follow you to your apartment."

THE MOON FLIRTED with the clouds as Jill drove her van back to her apartment. She rolled down the windows in the van and let the warm, pine-scented night air blow in. She turned up the radio. She couldn't remember ever being this happy. Not even the day Trevor asked her to marry him.

When she parked, she saw that she had company. Brenna was waiting anxiously on her doorstep.

"I'm so glad to see you," Brenna said. "I have to tell you—" She stopped abruptly when she saw Mac pull up behind the van and get out of his truck.

Jill figured whatever her friend had found out must be about him.

"Mac, this is my friend Brenna Margaret Boyd. Brenna, Mackenzie Cooper."

Mac's smile had an edge to it. "Mac. But we've met. Last night at the Beach Bar." He shot Jill a look that said he had only suspected he'd been set up the night before—but was well aware of it now. He shook Brenna's hand, then glanced at Jill. "Let's go up to your apartment, and then I'll have a look around."

Brenna looked as if she was bursting to tell Jill something, but asked first, when Mac left the room, "What happened last night on the boat?"

Jill filled her in, skipping the part about the skull. Nor did she tell Brenna about the ring Trevor had given her. Both stories were too big for a reporter to sit on, and Jill didn't want to put her friend in that position. When Mac found out from his friend whether or not the skull was that of one of the missing teenaged girls, then Jill would tell Brenna and let her go after the story.

"*He* was your mystery lover?" Brenna cried.

Jill shushed her. "I've never felt like this."

"You do look flushed and a little wild-eyed," her friend said. "Jill, you know nothing about this man!"

"I know everything I need to know." Jill saw Brenna look uncomfortable. "Don't I?"

Mac rejoined them. "I've checked all the locks and windows in both the apartment and bakery—"

His cell phone rang. He held Jill's gaze for a moment, then answered it.

"Uncle Mac?"

"Shane." Mac took a relieved breath, fighting the urge to yell at his nephew. "Where are you?"

"I'm in trouble."

As if Mac didn't know that.

"I need your help." The fear he heard in Shane's voice scared him. "I think someone's trying to kill me." Shane sounded close to tears.

"Tell me where you are," Mac ordered. He looked up to see Jill watching him, looking concerned.

"I'm at the gas station phone booth at Yellow Bay, but I can't stay here," Shane said.

"All right. Just tell me where to meet you."

"Do you know where that abandoned cherry-packing plant is near Finley Point?"

Mac remembered passing it earlier that day on the way out to Marvin Dodd's. "Yes. I'll be there in just a few minutes. Shane?"

"Yes?"

"Be careful."

He hung up and looked at Jill.

"Go," she said. "I'll be fine."

"I'll stay with her," Brenna said.

Mac couldn't take his eyes off Jill. He didn't want to leave her, but she was much safer here than where he was headed. "Lock up behind me. I'll be back as soon as I can."

She nodded and followed him down the stairs.

"She seems like a good friend," he said, knowing Brenna was waiting for Jill upstairs and, from the looks of her, dying to talk to Jill alone.

"She is a good friend."

He nodded, wanting to pull Jill into his arms, wanting to kiss her. "You have a good life here." Kissing her would mess up that life.

She looked as if she might cry. "Be careful?"

He touched her cheek, then turned and left before he said something he couldn't take back. Something that could change his life. Forever.

JILL WATCHED Mac leave. He'd looked worried. About his nephew? Or was he worried about what Brenna might tell her? She wanted to believe it was because he cared more than he wanted to admit.

She'd wanted him to kiss her. For a moment at the door, she thought he might. But she knew if he did, she'd only want more.

When she got back upstairs, Brenna was pacing. "Okay, what is it you're dying to tell me?"

"He was married."

"Mac?"

"They met his last year in college."

"And?"

"And she died. Cancer."

Jill sat down. "Oh, how awful. She must have been very young."

Brenna nodded. "They'd been living in Denver, but he left right after that. The people he worked with at a private-investigations office there said he was devastated by his wife's death. His whole personality changed. He started keeping to himself, moving a lot and became bitter and cynical. I guess he avoids relationships big time."

"That explains why he seems so...afraid of what happened between us. So determined it won't happen again."

"Maybe it shouldn't," Brenna said.

Jill sighed. "I don't know. I just know that what happened between us wasn't just great sex. Something clicked, something...big. And I'm afraid this sort of thing only comes along once in a lifetime. I don't want to pass it up. I want to see where it takes me."

"What about Mac?" Brenna asked.

"He's determined to keep me at arm's length." The phone rang, making Jill jump. She went to answer it, worried about Mac and Shane.

It was her father. "I'm fine," she told him. "Brenna is here with me. Catch any fish?"

"We got a few."

We? "Who went with you?" she asked.

Silence. "Darlene. I've been wanting the two of you to meet." Silence.

Jill felt tears burn her eyes. She'd caught the sound of happiness in her father's voice. "I would love to meet her." She could almost feel his relief over the phone line.

"Oh, Jill, I can't tell you how glad that makes me."

She was crying softly. "Dad, I like it that you've found someone. I don't want you to be sad anymore."

"I'll see you in the morning, then," he said. "Sleep tight, sweetheart."

"You too, Dad."

As Jill hung up, she dried her tears and noticed the answering machine blinking. She pushed Play and was startled to hear the other Scarlett's voice. Only, there was another layer to it. Fear.

"It's Rachel. I have to talk to you." She was whispering as if she thought someone might be listening in. "Call me. It's urgent." She left a cellphone number.

When Jill looked up, Brenna was standing in the doorway. "Our missing Rachel? She sounds scared."

Jill nodded. According to the answering machine, Rachel had called shortly after the funeral this morning. Jill dialed the number, her fingers shaking. As horrible as the woman had been to her after the funeral, what could she possibly want to talk to her about?

The phone rang and rang. Jill was about to hang

up when someone picked up. She could hear breathing on the line and held the phone so Brenna could listen, too.

"Rachel? It's Jill."

Silence. Then, Rachel crying, her voice breaking. "He's going to kill me. Oh, God. I need money to get out of town. You have to help me. No cops."

"Who?"

No answer.

"I lost him, but he knows the cops are looking for me. If they find me, he'll know." She was crying harder now.

"Where are you?"

"Waterside. Hurry." The line disconnected.

The old Waterside Campground was down the lake road about twenty miles. It hadn't been open in years. Jill looked at her watch, then at Brenna.

"You told Mac you wouldn't leave," her friend reminded her.

"I have to go. You heard her. She seems to think whoever is after her has some connection to the police," Jill said, remembering how Arnie had found out about her mystery lover through his cousin at city hall. "The killer might have a scanner."

Brenna nodded. "I still don't like this."

"I don't, either, but you heard her. She's scared and in trouble. If I send the sheriff's deputies, the killer could get to her first."

"Well, I'm going with you," Brenna said. "Better leave a note for Mac."

Jill and Brenna climbed into The Best Buns in Town van and started down the lake road. Only occasionally did the moon peek through the clouds. A cold, damp blackness had settled in and the air smelled of rain.

They left Bigfork behind. There was little traffic this time of the night and this late in the summer. The pines gave way to cherry orchards and long stretches of nothing but trees and darkness.

Just past an abandoned orchard, the right front tire on the van blew.

Chapter Thirteen

Jill gripped the steering wheel, fighting to keep the van on the narrow road as she braked to a stop. Fortunately she hadn't been going fast, but then, she couldn't on this stretch of the highway.

At a wide spot she pulled off the road, the tire thumping, the van listing forward and to the right.

"I can't believe we have a blowout now," Brenna said as she climbed out with the flashlight from the glove compartment.

Jill got out, glanced at the flat, right-front tire and went around to the back of the van to get the jack. She was digging it out when she heard Brenna say, "That's funny. The tire has a hole in it. Almost looks like a bullet hole."

"A bullet hole? Like someone shot it?" Jill hauled the jack to the front of the van but didn't see her friend. The flashlight lay on the ground by the tire. "Brenna?" A cold wind blew off the water. The dark pines swayed, the limbs moaning softly.

Where had she gone? Jill looked down at the flat tire, saw the perfect hole in the sidewall and felt a chill. "Brenna?" She stared up and down the road and saw nothing but darkness. On either side of the pavement the bare limbs of the abandoned orchard were etched black against the night. "Brenna!" Her voice was lost in the wind.

Jill put down the jack and walked around to the driver's side of the van, fighting the urge to run. Brenna wouldn't just walk off. Someone had shot out the tire. Someone had taken Brenna. Someone was still out there.

Her hands shaking, she hurriedly climbed in and reached for her purse with her cell phone inside. It wasn't between the seats where she'd left it.

Get out of here! Fear made her limbs numb, useless, her movements slow. She could still drive on a flat. To get help she would do whatever she had to. She reached to turn on the ignition.

The keys were gone!

Her pulse pounded. Behind her, she heard the whisper of a sound and for just an instant thought it might be Brenna. Her gaze flew to the rearview mirror. She saw a pair of eyes glittering from a black ski mask as a man lunged at her.

A gloved hand brushed her arm, but didn't find purchase as she threw open the van door and jumped out.

The moment her feet hit the pavement, she took off at a run, remembering another night long ago when she'd done the same on this very road.

She heard her assailant come crashing out of the back of the van. She ran down the middle of the road, knowing she didn't stand a chance of disappearing into the stark trees of the old cherry orchard, nor could she run down the steep mountainside.

She didn't dare look back as she ran up the long incline, praying a car would come along. Her side ached and her legs felt numb. On one side tall pines made a dark wall along the edge of the narrow road. On the opposite side the land fell away, dropping radically the half mile down to the lake.

In the distance she thought she heard the sound of a car engine. Suddenly the glare of headlights blinded her as a vehicle came up over the rise in the road, answering her prayers. She could hear the roar of the engine. She waved her arms frantically. "Stop! Please help me!"

THE OLD CHERRY-PACKING plant loomed up from the road, dark and massive against the night sky. Mac cut the lights and engine, coasting to a stop fifty yards away.

He waited for a moment, letting his eyes adjust to the dark, then he quietly opened his door and stepped out, pulling his weapon from his ankle holster as he headed toward the building.

He hadn't gone far when he saw movement. Shane stepped out of the shadows.

"Uncle Mac, man, he's trying to kill me."

Mac motioned for Shane to be quiet until they reached the truck. The kid loped along beside him, looking over his shoulder, obviously scared.

Once back in the pickup, Mac holstered his weapon, started the engine and headed back to town, keeping an eye on his rearview mirror. "Okay, let's hear it."

"It wasn't my fault."

"It never is." Mac was glad he was driving or he might have torn the kid limb from limb. "Tell me about the coins."

"Trevor ordered Marvin and me to be ready one night. We didn't know we were going to *rob* someone. I'm telling you the truth. And I think there was something else in that metal box beside those coins."

"Like what?" Mac asked.

"I don't know, man. Something that got Trevor killed."

"Did you have anything to do with Trevor's death?" Mac asked, shooting a look at his nephew. "Don't lie to me, Shane."

"No way, man! No way!"

Mac let out a sigh. "There was a surveillance camera that caught you on tape. You, Trevor and Marvin. Who was the other guy? The one who was inside during the burglary?"

Shane looked scared. "I think that's the dude that's been trying to kill me."

"What's his name?" Mac said, losing patience.

"Arnie. Arnie Evans. He was Trevor's best friend, but I gotta tell you, I think he killed Trevor." Shane was nodding. "I know it sounds crazy, them being best friends and all, but I think the dude killed him, man."

As JILL WAVED her arms, the car came to a screeching halt just feet from her in the middle of the lake road. She shielded her eyes, trying to see past the bright headlights. "Please, help me!" she cried again, hearing the hysteria in her voice.

"Jill?"

Arnie? She rushed to the driver's side of the car. "Oh, thank God, Arnie. There's someone…" She looked back down the road toward the van. No one was behind her. "Brenna. I can't find Brenna. And there was this man—"

"Get in," Arnie said, turning his headlights to bright. The van, back down the road a short distance, was visible in the light, its right-front tire flat. There was no movement around it. Just darkness. "Hurry," Arnie said.

She ran around the front of the car to the passenger side. Arnie already had the door open. She leaped in and slammed the door after her. She heard the click of the automatic lock.

"We…we had a flat. Brenna got out to look and then…" Jill was gasping for air, her heart hammering and her body shaking so hard she was having trouble speaking. "Someone shot out the tire and now Brenna is gone and there was this man in the back of the van…"

"Easy," Arnie said.

"He was wearing a black ski mask. We have to look for Brenna. Where's your cell phone? We have to call for help."

"I don't have a cell phone." He let the black sports car coast slowly down the hill past the van, his expression grim. "You're sure you saw a man in a black ski mask?"

"Yes." Why wasn't he asking about Brenna? Why wasn't he racing into town for help? "Arnie, we have to get to town. We have to get help." She started to cry. "I'm so afraid something terrible has happened to Brenna."

As they passed the van, she saw that both its back doors were open, the dome light was on, and it was empty.

Arnie looked down the road and suddenly spun the sports car around highway-patrol style and started back up the hill he'd just come down.

"Where are you going?" she cried. "Town's the other way."

He glanced in his rearview mirror and swore. "There was someone waiting for us down the road."

"I don't see anyone," she said, looking back.

"Someone's following us with his headlights turned off." Arnie sounded scared as he sped up.

She swiveled around in the seat to look back, but saw nothing but darkness.

"We have to try to lose him," Arnie said. "Hang on."

She buckled up her seat belt. "Arnie, I don't see anyone back there. Please, turn around. Let's go back to town to the sheriff's department. If there really is someone following us—"

"We'd never reach town," he said as he pushed the gas pedal to the floor. The sports car took off, pressing her back against the seat. The car shot down the road, the tires squealing as he took the curves of the narrow, steep road, driving farther and farther away from town—and help.

Arnie glanced in the rearview mirror again and swore. "He's staying right with us." In the dash lights, she could see beads of sweat on his forehead, his knuckles white on the steering wheel, his eyes wild.

"Arnie, what are you doing?"

"This is the only way," he said, his voice breaking with emotion. "This is all Trevor's fault. I hope he's burning in hell." The bitterness in his voice shocked her. "You can't imagine the things I did for him. The secrets I kept. I should have known I couldn't trust him."

Her heart jumped to her throat. Oh, my God. She was shaking her head, telling herself this wasn't happening.

"And now I'm the one who has to pay the price. He took Rachel from me after taking my father's last dime. It killed him, you know, losing everything." He looked in the rearview mirror again. Fear seemed to deform his face. She could hear him breathing heavily.

She started to turn in her seat to look back again to see if anyone was following them, but suddenly Arnie hit the brakes. The sports car went into a sideways skid in the middle of the road, tires screeching, smoke billowing. She could see out over an old cherry orchard, see the lake way down at the bottom of the steep mountainside past the orchard.

Jill let out a scream as Arnie hit the gas. The

sports car leaped forward and then dropped over the edge of the pavement. For a moment she thought he'd lost his mind. But then the tires came down hard on a dirt road that cut through the trees of the orchard and down the mountain.

Jill felt as if she was falling as the sports car roared down through the tunnel of trees, the headlights flickering on the dark green of the branches, dust boiling up behind them.

Clinging to the door handle, she shot a look at Arnie. His face looked feral in the dash lights, eyes wild, teeth bared as he wrestled the wheel, fighting to keep the car on the dirt road between the trees.

Moonlight flickered through the clouds, and she saw the lake coming up fast—and the cliff at the end of the road, dropping to the water below.

"Arnie, don't do this! For God's sake!"

But Arnie didn't slow. In fact, he kept the gas pedal to the floor. "This is the only way."

"My God, what are you doing?" she cried over the roar of the engine.

The car continued on down, the cherry trees blurring past. Her pulse thrummed in her ears.

"I told Trevor," Arnie said. "Please don't get my dad involved in any of your schemes. I begged him. 'No, buddy, I wouldn't take a chance with your old man's retirement. Come on, what kind of guy do you think I am?'" The perfect mimic of Trevor's voice startled her. "I trusted him. My dad invested everything, thinking Trevor was going to make him rich. It killed him. When he realized he'd lost everything, his heart couldn't take it. All those years of working under some guy's car, grease under his fingernails, all those years…''

The limbs of trees smacked the windshield and scraped the roof loudly.

''Trevor deserved to die.'' Arnie went on. ''He got what was coming to him.''

A weapon. She had to stop him. She grabbed for the wheel and he backhanded her, knocking her against the door. She reached the latch on the glove compartment. The compartment door flopped down, spilling everything. A black ski mask tumbled out and landed on the floor at her feet.

''It was you,'' she whispered hoarsely, then looked up to see that they were about to go over the cliff and plunge into the lake below.

At the last minute, Arnie turned the wheel and hit the brakes. Jill saw the cherry trees coming at her. A large branch hit the windshield, shattering it. She could hear the limbs slamming into the car, feel the car start to roll in the soft earth between the trees, then flatten out, still moving.

When at last the car stopped, Arnie threw open his door and stumbled out. Shaken, she groped for her door handle, pulled it. The door fell open and she was out and running almost before her feet hit the ground.

She heard the pounding of his feet behind her. He was close, very close. She could hear his ragged breath, almost feel it on her neck.

She stumbled and almost fell. She felt the brush of his hand through her hair and dodged to the right. The wrong way. It led to the cliff.

He tackled her and took her down hard, knocking the breath out of her as they fell. He quickly got up, dragging her to her feet and pulling her toward the cliff—and the lake below.

"This is the only way out," he said as she tried to fight him with her fists and kicked at him.

"No!" she screamed. It couldn't end like this. Mackenzie Cooper's face flashed in her mind and she cried out for him.

His arm around her chest, his free hand covering her mouth, Arnie dragged her the few yards to the edge of the cliff.

They teetered on the rim and she looked down, feeling the cold, wet air blowing up from the water. She thought she saw a light below her in the water, but realized it was lightning—a storm was approaching. Thunder rumbled somewhere out on the lake. Just like the night Trevor was murdered.

She tried to stop Arnie, but he was too strong. He picked her up and held her out over the edge of the cliff, out over the water, then he swung her body outward and released her.

She grabbed for him, got nothing but air. In that microsecond, she hung, suspended at eye level with him as lightning lit the sky around her. She thought she glimpsed regret in his expression. Sorrow. He teetered on the edge of the cliff as if to jump, then turned to look back, his face twisting in terror as if he saw Trevor's ghost behind him.

Then Jill was falling. She hit the water, the force of her fall driving her deep into the cold darkness of the lake.

At first she saw nothing, felt only the all-encompassing liquid prison. Then she saw light above her. Her lungs screaming for air, she started to swim toward the surface, toward the shaft of light that sliced through the clear water.

She made the mistake of looking down and saw the source of the light. A car rested at an angle on the bottom, its headlights shining upward through the water.

The driver's-side door was open, the dome light on, the driver still behind the wheel, her hair floating around her face like a dark aura.

Jill let out a cry, swallowing water, losing critical air. Frantically, she swam toward the surface, following the shaft of light pointing upward from her red Saturn's headlights, the image of Rachel Wells bound to the steering wheel with duct tape branded on her brain.

As she neared the surface, she saw Arnie's body above her, the water dark around him, the side of his head smashed in.

She kicked away from him and broke the surface at last, gasping for air, choking on the lake water she'd swallowed, choking on the fear that still clutched at her chest.

From above her, Jill thought she heard someone cry her name. She swam toward the rocky shore, praying she wasn't imagining the sound of Mac's voice.

Chapter Fourteen

It was late afternoon by the time the sheriff let Mac go into Jill's hospital room. He stopped just inside the door, shocked at the sight of her lying on the bed, so small, so pale. White as the sheets around her. Her eyes were closed, her lashes dark against her cheeks. His chest constricted at the sight of her.

He'd been so wrong. So very wrong. He closed his eyes as the pain and anger engulfed him, recalling what he'd read in the sheriff's report from Jill and Brenna's statements.

The sheriff had concluded that it had been Arnie who'd killed Trevor. After all the years of taking everything that Trevor dished out, Arnie had finally had enough when Trevor stole Rachel from him. He blamed Trevor for his father's heart attack, as well, but Rachel, it seemed, had been the last straw.

The sheriff had found evidence that led him to conclude that Arnie had also killed Rachel. But not before she'd made the call to Jill, which had brought Jill and Brenna down the lake road to meet her. Arnie must have been lying in wait. He shot the tire out on the van, attacked Brenna, then, wearing the black ski mask Jill had found in his glove compartment, gone after Jill.

When she'd gotten away and run, it was believed he must have gone to his car and come back, pretending he just happened on to her.

By the time Charley Johnson had called from the Kalispell Police Department to say that the skull was a positive match for a teenaged girl who'd disappeared nine years ago, the case was already closed.

More of the dead teenagers' jewelry had turned up in a safety-deposit box Trevor Forester kept at the bank.

Trevor was believed to have killed all eleven girls over the years. Arnie Evans was dead now, too. The coroner concluded that Arnie had hit his head when he fell from the cliff and was dead by the time he hit the water. Jill was just lucky to have survived.

"Mac?" She opened her eyes as if sensing him in the room.

He tried to smile. It hurt. As he moved to the side of her bed, he had the same feeling of failure he'd had when his wife, Emily, had died of cancer. Helpless. The pain excruciating. Unbearable. He'd promised himself he would never care that much again.

"I'm so sorry," he said, taking her hand. Her skin was surprisingly warm. He tried to think of the right words, but he knew there weren't any. He'd failed this woman. Failed himself. Worse, his feelings for her were killing him. "If I hadn't left you and Brenna..."

She shook her head. "You had to help Shane. I

was the fool, taking off the way I did. Thank God, Brenna's all right.''

He nodded. Arnie had only knocked Brenna out and dragged her into the pine trees. She'd suffered a slight concussion and a few scrapes and bruises.

''I know why you're here,'' Jill said, her gaze locking with his. ''You came to say goodbye.''

He nodded, unable to speak.

She smiled, her eyes filling with tears. ''It hurts to care so much about someone. I understand that. I understand why you can't let yourself do it again.''

So she knew about Emily.

''I guess you heard—Shane and Zoe have decided to go to college together,'' she said. ''They're going to the junior college in Kalispell, so Zoe can still work part-time at the bakery. They're in love.''

''Yeah.'' He let go of her hand and stepped back. ''I'd better go.'' There was so much he wasn't saying. Couldn't say. Best left unsaid. And yet it was hard to leave. As he turned and walked to the door of her room, opened it and went to step through, he couldn't help himself. He glanced back.

His eyes met hers, all the feeling they'd felt that first night arcing like lightning across the room, warming him to his center. And then he left and the door closed behind him.

MAC HAD ONE STOP to make on his way out of town.

Nathaniel Pierce greeted him. ''I figured you'd be by today.'' He motioned Mac inside. ''Do you have time for a drink? Or do you just want your pay before you leave?''

He grinned at Mac's obvious surprise. "Summer's almost gone. Your job's over. Nothing can keep you here now. Not even a woman. Not even Jill Lawson, it seems."

Mac took the last two twenty-dollar gold pieces from his pocket and held them out to the man. "That makes all twelve, right?"

Pierce nodded slowly as he took the coins from him. "I guess that concludes our business. Now, about that drink…" He walked to the bar in the massive living room and filled two glasses from a decanter.

Mac watched him. "I know why you hired me," he said as Pierce offered him the drink. "You already had ten of the coins back and you could have gotten the other two as easily as I did. Probably more easily. But you didn't want Marvin or Shane. You wanted that fourth man. The shadow on the videotape you said you didn't notice."

Pierce held out one of the filled glasses. Mac took it and watched Pierce walk over to a small antique desk. He opened a drawer, took out a check, closed the drawer and crossed to Mac to hand him the check.

Mac took it and glanced at the amount. More than triple what he normally charged. "I know you killed them—Trevor, Rachel, Arnie. I can't prove it, but I know you did."

Pierce lifted his glass as if in salute, then took a sip. "Greed killed them."

"If greed killed, you'd never have been born," Mac said, putting down his untouched drink. He tore up the check and let the pieces fall to the highly glossed hardwood floor. Then he turned and walked out of the house.

He headed his truck down the lake road away from Flathead, away from Jill, telling himself he was doing her a favor by leaving. But he hadn't gotten far when he realized just how wrong he'd been. He slowed the truck, feeling a pull on him stronger than any he could remember.

Damn. He had to go back.

His cell phone rang. He clicked it on, thinking it might be Jill, disappointed when it wasn't. It was a friend he'd called about Pierce's gold coins. Mac had been curious just how much three lives were worth.

"Those dates you gave me of the two coins," his friend said. "Those are worth about two hundred bucks apiece."

"What?" Mac said, braking and pulling off the road. "I guess I should have told you. They're part of a twelve-coin set."

"Wouldn't make any difference. Those are common years. Even if you had the missing years, they'd all be worth about two hundred bucks, or about fourteen hundred dollars in total."

Mac felt his pulse pound. "You're sure?"

"You wouldn't have called me if you didn't think I knew my coins," his friend said. "Anyway, I have the book right in front of me."

Mac thanked him and clicked off, then floored the pickup. Pierce had lied. Mac wasn't sure why that surprised him. The coins weren't rare. So what the hell had getting them back been about? Just simple vengeance?

Mac remembered what Shane had said about Arnie thinking there was more in the metal box than just the coins and if there had been something else, Trevor had it. His heart leaped to his throat. Oh, God, he had to be wrong.

BRENNA CAME IN shortly after Mac left Jill's hospital room. "I heard they were releasing you and I figured you'd need a ride home."

"He's gone," Jill said, and finally let the tears come.

Brenna rushed to her. "Oh, sweetie." She hugged Jill, gently rocking her.

The nurse came in and shooed Brenna away, saying Jill needed her rest. The sleeping pill gave her nightmares. Or maybe the nightmares were just from the past few days and everything that had happened.

Jill awoke with a start a couple of hours later, and for a moment she thought Mac was in the room with her again. He wasn't. He was gone. Gone from her life. Leaving her empty inside and lonelier than she'd ever been, mourning what could have been.

The doctor released her, and Brenna drove her to the bakery. Zoe and Shane were there, along with Jill's father and his woman friend Darlene and a bunch of Jill's friends, all gathered to welcome her home.

Although seeing them lifted her spirits, she still felt empty inside, as if some part of her had left with

Mac. Darlene had baked a cake, which she cut and which Zoe served with coffee.

Darlene was petite and gray-haired, with twinkling blue eyes and a cheery disposition. Perfect for Jill's father.

The phone rang every few minutes. Jill didn't feel like talking to anyone right now and asked her father to take messages. People were calling to wish her well. Other calls were from reporters from other newspapers wanting interviews, he said.

Jill looked through the array of flowers and cards that had been sent. Many of them were from her regular customers. She was deeply touched.

"This one has a note on it that says you have to read the card before eight-fifteen," Darlene said, and glanced at her watch. "You're barely going to make it."

Eight-fifteen? Jill took the card from the large bouquet of red roses, hope soaring through her as she ripped open the envelope and read:

> I can't leave you. Meet me tonight at the cottage at 8:15 unless you're too smart to get involved with a man like me.
>
>   Mac

Jill began to cry.

"Is it bad news?" Darlene asked, sounding concerned.

Jill hugged her. "No, it's wonderful news."

Zoe came up and read the card over her shoulder.

"Too cool," she said. "You'd better get moving or you're gonna be late. Take my car."

MAC FLOORED the gas. It hadn't been about the coins. Or revenge.

His breath escaped in a rush. "No." He'd felt from the first that everything about this was wrong. He'd known. On some level, he'd known.

Pierce had his coins. Shane said he thought something else was in the box. But whatever it had been, Trevor must have taken it.

The sheriff's report. Jill's words: "Arnie said someone was after him, trying to kill him. He'd seemed so afraid."

But she hadn't seen anyone and in the end concluded Arnie had just pretended they were being chased so he could get her to the same spot where he'd killed Rachel Wells. But Mac knew better now. Arnie had been trying to save Jill by throwing her into the lake.

Arnie hadn't fallen or jumped. Pierce had probably struck him with something. If Mac hadn't gotten to Jill when he did, if he hadn't seen the skid marks on the road, then the van with the flat, if he hadn't gone back to the skid marks, driven down through the orchard…

Mac watched the headlights eat up the pavement.

He dialed the hospital. Jill had already been released. He called her home number. No answer. He dialed information. Got her father's number. No answer there, either. Information gave him Zoe's number. The phone rang and rang, and finally it was picked up. He could hear rock music. "Zoe?"

The music stopped with a suddenness that was both comforting and jarring.

"Hello," she said with a giggle, her attention obviously elsewhere. Shane must have been with her.

"Do you know where Jill is?" he asked.

"Mac? She went to meet you."

What? "Meet me?"

"Yeah, she got the note you sent with the flowers."

He'd never sent a woman flowers in his life. Not even Emily. He wished now that he had. That he'd had the sense to send them to Jill with a note telling her to meet him.

"Where was she meeting me?"

Zoe let out another giggle. "You should know."

"Where?"

"At the Foresters' lake cottage."

He hung up. He wasn't far from the Foresters'. He could be there faster than the sheriff's department could get there. And unlike the deputies, Mac knew what to expect when he got there.

As she stepped into the dark cottage a little before eight-fifteen, Jill sensed Mac near her—just as she had that first time. Only now something was different. At first she didn't know what. Then she caught the faint scent of his aftershave.

Mac hadn't worn aftershave that first night. In fact, she couldn't remember ever smelling it when he was around her. He always smelled of soap and sunshine.

"Mac?" Her voice sounded tight, nervous even to her. She heard the scuff of shoes on the tile floor. He was close. Close enough he could touch her. She felt a chill, a combination of desire. And fear. Something felt wrong. She'd been so excited that Mac had come back. Excited he'd wanted to make love again in the cottage. That he'd changed his mind about the two of them.

She stepped back, banging into the door she'd just closed behind her. "Mac?" The urgency in her voice seemed only to send her fear escalating. "Turn on a light. You're scaring me."

There was a whisper of sound in the pitch blackness, then a light flared from the corner, momentarily blinding her.

She blinked. "You're not Mac." She was feeling for the door handle behind her, her blood pounding in her ears, and yet she was telling herself there was no reason to be afraid.

The man before her was no homeless person off the street. In fact, he looked as if he belonged here. He wore gray jeans, a white polo shirt and deck shoes, and he was sprawled in a chair, a glass of red wine next to him on the end table.

"Sorry if I scared you," he said. He seemed amused, rather than upset, that she'd just walked into the cottage. "I'm a friend of Alistair's. I'm staying here tonight, keeping an eye on the place. I was just enjoying watching the lake in the dark," he said as if anticipating her question, and smiled.

"I can see you're disappointed that I'm not this Mac you were looking for. Sorry."

She was the one who was sorry. And confused. Where was Mac?

The man rose gracefully from the chair. "I don't think we've ever met." He held out his hand. "I'm Nathaniel Pierce and you, I know, are Jill Lawson." His smile broadened at her surprise. "I've seen you around and heard volumes from Alistair. He's quite a fan of yours."

She tried to relax, but felt strung tight as piano wire as she reached for his hand. She told herself it was from her disappointment. Her surprise to find someone other than Mac in the cottage. In the dark.

His larger hand enveloped hers and she felt a jolt of something like…fear. Her gaze flew up to his. She knew she'd never met him before, but something about Nathaniel Pierce seemed familiar. "I should be going." She tried to free her hand, but he held on to it.

"So soon? What if your…Mac shows up? Why don't you join me in a glass of wine while we wait for him?" His gaze held hers as securely as his hand trapped hers in his.

"No, thank you. Maybe he's waiting for me by the house."

"I wouldn't be so sure about that, Jill."

A shaft of ice cut down her spine at the change in his voice. She'd heard the voice before. Her heart hammered in her ears. He was pulling on her wrist— just as he had fourteen years ago that night beside the lake road. The night he'd tried to give her a ride.

"No!" She brought her free hand down hard on his wrist, breaking his hold, and bolted for the door. But he was right behind her. He hit the door with his palms, slamming it shut with a thud, one hand on each side of her.

"Did you like the roses?" he whispered.

She didn't breathe. Didn't move.

"You know, I'd forgotten about you," he said in that same whisper. "It had been so many years. You were the only one who got away. Really messed up my summer. Quite a few of my summers. I had to leave after that, get rid of that car. I did love that car."

She remembered the car and him. It had taken her years before she could sleep without a night-light because of him.

The realization made her fear spike. It hadn't been Trevor who killed those teenaged girls. And those years when no girls had disappeared were when Nathaniel had been gone. Her legs were jelly. She had trouble taking her next breath. There was no one around but them. No one to hear her scream. Nathaniel Pierce had killed all those girls. She'd been the only one to get away.

And now he'd caught her.

"I didn't know who'd robbed me until Heddy was telling me about the antique ring Trevor had bought you. She knew I'd always been interested in jewelry and had some expertise—I'd taken enough of it off girls' dead bodies." He laughed, a bloodcurdling sound. "Heddy wanted to know what it was worth. She was probably wondering where her son had gotten the money for such a ring. I almost laughed in her face.''

He pressed Jill closer against the door with his body, his face next to hers. ''I asked what other presents her dear son had given you. She told me about the silver charm bracelet. She thought it was sweet. *Sweet.* The bastard was giving you jewelry that belonged to my girls, the jewelry I'd taken off their bodies after I'd...enjoyed their youth, their innocence, their last moments of life.''

She shuddered.

''What else did Trevor give you from my stash?''

She shook her head.

''Don't lie.''

It had been dark that night when the car stopped to pick her up. She hadn't really noticed it—nor had she seen the driver's face in the dark. Later she recalled there was no light inside the car when he'd stopped for her. He had turned off the dash lights. He would need to work in the dark.

He crushed his body against her. She could feel him reaching for something. The next thing she knew, he slapped a wet rag over her mouth and nose. She fought the smell. She fought him. But not for long.

JILL AWOKE to a blinding white light. The pain in her head assured her she was not dead. That and the rock of the boat and the sound of him breathing over her.

She closed her eyes tightly as the light moved closer and she felt his hands on her again. It wasn't until he'd lifted her in his arms and carried her out of the boat that she opened her eyes and saw that he wore a headlamp.

As she followed its beam, she saw where he'd brought her. Her heart dropped like a stone.

The old mansion on the island stood stark against the night sky. Suddenly she couldn't get enough air through her nostrils. She began to panic, her breathing shallow. Tiny flecks of light danced before her eyes. She was going to pass out again.

He stopped, shifted her in his arms to free one of his hands and ripped the tape from her mouth.

She gasped at the pain and began taking large gulps of night air. Sobs rose from her panic and she was crying and gasping.

He carried her up some stairs, the steps groaning under them from the weight. The smell hit her first. Rotting decay. Then the whine of the wind as it moved restlessly through the empty structure.

She'd feared where he was taking her the moment she'd seen the house. All the years of hearing the stories about Aria Hillinger. Her beauty. Her tragic life. And worse, her tragic death. The stories about people hearing a woman's screams coming from the island. Jill's blood turned to ice when she realized those had been real screams over the years. Young women who'd been carried up these same stairs to their deaths.

He put her down on the edge of the fourth-floor balcony, but his hand remained on her neck, his fingers biting into her flesh. The railing was gone.

Jill was so close to the edge she could feel the

wind blowing up the side of the house into her face. All he had to do was straighten his arm and let go of her neck and she would be airborne. This time, the fall would kill her because she would land in the rocks below, not in the water. Not in the water as she had when Arnie had thrown her off the cliff. Oh, God, Arnie. It had been Pierce after him. Arnie had saved her life.

The wind blew back her hair, stole her breath. She tried not to panic. Tried to think. But she knew as she teetered precariously on the edge of the deck that she stood no chance of besting this man physically.

It was clear he had stood here many times before. That alone terrified her. How many other women had stood here, knowing they were going to die? Jill could feel their fear as keenly as she could feel the evil inside these walls. Women had screamed for their lives. Just as she would scream for hers.

MAC REACHED the cottage, saw Zoe's Beetle parked near the Foresters' dark house. No other cars. Pierce must have come by boat.

Mac was out of the pickup, running down the hill to the cottage, knowing he was too late when he saw the dock empty. He burst into the cottage, anyway. Would Pierce expect him to come back? Mac doubted it. Pierce thought he knew him so well. Pierce thought he would run from a woman like Jill Lawson as fast as his pickup would take him.

No, Pierce wouldn't expect him.

The cottage was empty—except for Jill's purse.

Mac picked it up, held it to his face, the soft leather smelling of her perfume.

Why had Pierce left her purse behind? For the same reason he'd sent the roses and note? To make everyone think Jill had gone to the cottage to meet Mac? When she disappeared, the sheriff would be looking for Mac—not Pierce.

He rushed out to the dock. He and Pierce had stolen a few cars in their youth. Hot-wiring a boat would be a piece of cake. He jumped into the fastest of the Forester boats. Within minutes he was roaring across the water, headed for the island. He'd remembered something Pierce had told him about his mother one night when he'd been drunk and his defenses down. The next morning he'd sworn it was a lie.

But even then Mac had heard a ring of truth in Pierce's story.

"Katherine isn't my real mother. My real mother killed herself when she was young," Pierce had said. "Really young. My father doesn't think I remember her, but I do. I used to stand on the balcony with her. I used to worry that she would try to jump. She could never have reached the water from the fourth story."

"Did she jump?" Mac had asked.

"No. She hung herself."

JILL HEARD Nathaniel Pierce take a breath and watched him look out at the lake as he began to speak. It was some sort of a ritual, she thought.

"She was so beautiful," he said. "Childlike. She

used to stand here and look out at the lake. She loved this room. I would stand here with her. Her hair was long and blond and she smelled of summer and something sweet like strawberries. Her arms were slim and she wore a bracelet my grandfather had given her. A tiny silver bracelet.''

Jill's throat closed. Aria Hillinger. My God, he was talking about Aria Hillinger. Goosebumps skittered over her bare skin. Nathaniel Pierce had been the child. The child believed to have drowned or starved to death on this island.

''She loved me,'' Pierce said. ''She was so sweet and innocent. You would see it in her eyes, as if her life was just beginning and nothing could hurt her.''

He looked at Jill and she knew the ritual was almost over. Her fear spiked, a shot of adrenaline that sent her heart into overdrive.

Those other women, had they fought? Had they tried to talk him out of killing them? Had they believed that they could come up with a way out of this?

''He found me,'' Pierce said. ''My father. He'd finally come to save her, but it was too late. So he never told a soul. He was married, you see, to Katherine. So he brought me to her, made her lie. Katherine did anything my father told her. She pretended I was hers, hers and my father's. They just pretended my real mother never existed, that my father never had an affair…'' His voice trailed off, the silence even more frightening. ''But he bought up the island and all the Hillinger property.''

He seemed to come back as if from a distance.

"But I remember her. She was so beautiful. So young. Don't you see, she will always be young. My father is old now, a wrinkled, crippled-up old man who has suddenly developed a conscience. That's why he sold the island, you know. The old bastard knew what I'd been doing all these years but he didn't have the guts to try to stop me."

Pierce laughed, a horrible sound that held no humor. "He knew if anyone tried to develop this land, they would find the bodies. He was counting on that stopping me." Pierce shook his head, the headlamp swinging back and forth, making her stomach roil. "The old stupid fool. Now he is old and dying, but my mother will always be young. Just like you, Jill."

He began to take the tape off Jill's ankles. She watched him, gauging her chances of fighting him off physically once her hands were free. Bad plan. He was stronger, larger, and he'd obviously done this more times than she wanted to consider. She doubted anyone had gotten away from him. At least not for long.

"Of course, you will want to scream when the time comes," he said. "They all do."

She thought she heard a boat, but she couldn't see any lights. It sounded as if it was coming this way, fast. But Pierce didn't seem worried about it. He turned her around and that's when she saw the noose hanging from the rafters. He smiled at her surprise. "Let me tell you about asphyxiation," he said.

THE SOUND OF A BOAT grew closer. Still Nathaniel Pierce didn't seem to notice. Or care. Probably because no one came to the island, especially at night.

He dragged her over to the noose, the glare of his headlamp blinding her again. She tried to fight him—just as he'd obviously hoped. She heard a horrible sound and realized it was laughter. Nathaniel Pierce had thrown back his head and was laughing as he wrestled the noose around her neck.

The rope was coarse and chafed her skin. He tightened it around her throat, then stepped back to look at her as if posing her for a painting. Or a photograph.

Then he stepped close to her again, reached into his pocket and pulled out a silver charm bracelet with a tiny silver heart on it. He smiled with satisfaction as she saw the name engraved on it. Jill.

"It's yours," he said as he carefully clasped it on her wrist. "There, just as it should have been all those years ago. Fourteen, right?" His eyes sparkled.

She listened for the sound of the boat motor and realized she couldn't hear it anymore. Despair swept over her. The boat must have gone on past to the east side of the lake. She'd been praying that someone had seen the light from Pierce's headlamp. Would come to investigate.

But what fool would come to this island this late?

"Oh, you look so sad," Pierce said, lifting her chin with his finger and gazing at her face. "Just think, you will always be this age. Young. Not as young as you would have been fourteen years ago." He tsked. "Your own fault. You should have gotten into the car."

She tried to find her voice. If she could get him talking, she could buy herself a little precious time. "You killed Trevor, didn't you? And Rachel and Arnie and all those girls? Why?"

He shook his head as if disappointed in her, then walked over to where he'd tied the other end of the rope. She tried to run. To shake her head out of the noose. To get away.

He laughed again, clearly enjoying her delaying efforts. He pulled the rope. The noose tightened, then loosened again. "Are you sure you don't want to scream?"

She closed her eyes and thought of Mac, remembering their night in the cottage. She clung to that memory as Pierce jerked the rope tighter and tighter, lifting her off her feet. Mac was wrong. They would have been amazing together.

The rope cut into her neck, the pain excruciating. No air. She gasped, determined not to scream. Determined not to give Pierce that satisfaction, knowing it hadn't saved the other women he'd killed here, knowing it wasn't going to save her, either.

She could feel a different darkness. Stars glittered behind her lids. Then she heard it. The sound of footfalls thundering up the old wooden stairs. She opened her eyes.

Pierce had turned toward the sound, the headlamp shining on the landing at the top of the stairs.

Jill thought she only imagined Mac as he burst through the doorway, a gun in one hand, a flashlight in the other. She tried to call out to him, but the noose was too tight and she could feel herself passing out. She fought it with all her will. Don't give up now! Not now!

AT FIRST all Mac saw was the light shining at him. He dived to one side, expecting gunfire, and swept the beam of his flashlight across the room. The light wavered as it fell on Jill suspended above the floor, the noose around her neck.

Oh, my God! He was too late!

"Let her down!" he ordered, his voice breaking as he shone the beam of his flashlight on Pierce. "Let her down now!" He rushed over to Jill and lifted her, putting slack in the rope, all the while holding his gun on Pierce. But the man had tied the rope off and just stood watching as if with interest what Mac would do next.

"Untie the rope!" Mac yelled. "Or I'll blow your blue blood all over this room." He could feel a slight movement from Jill. She was alive!

"You don't want this woman or her mediocre life," Pierce said, the headlamp shining on Jill's face. "Why are you doing this? Can you imagine yourself making cinnamon rolls? She means nothing to you. Walk away, Mac. It's what you do best. Anyway, it's too late."

Mac put the first bullet in Pierce's right thigh. He let out a howl and dropped to one knee. "Untie the rope, Pierce. Now!" Mac's second shot only grazed Pierce's other thigh. Pierce stumbled over to the rope and quickly untied it.

Mac lowered Jill to the floor and, keeping his weapon close, loosened the noose around her neck until he could get it over her head. She gasped for breath and tried to speak.

"Shh, you're going to be all right," he said. "Don't talk. Just breathe."

She pulled Mac nearer. Her whisper was harsh and painful sounding, and he realized it took everything in her to get the words past her throat. "He has a gun."

The headlamp hadn't moved from the spot where Pierce had dropped after untying the rope. Mac flicked the beam of his flashlight to it and saw that the headlamp lay on the floor, the beam pointed at him. Pierce was gone!

Still on his knees beside Jill, Mac shone the flashlight across the room. Pierce couldn't have gotten away that quickly. Not wounded as he was. Mac would have heard him if he'd run. But Pierce hadn't run. He'd moved like a big cat, a cat with only one purpose—destroying its enemy. And Mac was that enemy, he realized as he felt the gun stab into his neck.

Pierce knocked the flashlight from Mac's hand. It hit the floor, the beam illuminating the three of them. Pierce squatted down next to Mac and eased the weapon from his fingers, then tossed it away into the darkness. Mac stared after it, memorizing where it was in case he got the chance to go after it.

Jill lay gasping on the floor, her hand to her throat, her eyes wide and terrified. Not for herself, but for him, Mac realized as Pierce leaned down.

"Why did you have to come back?" Pierce asked, squatting next to him, still pressing the barrel of the gun into his neck. "Why couldn't you just let this all end? She would have been my last, and then everything would have been forgotten."

"You're just kidding yourself, Pierce," Mac said, surprised by how calm he sounded. "You couldn't stop killing. Anyway, the cops know about the bodies you buried on this island. They're going to come after you."

Pierce laughed. "Nice try, old buddy, but they think Trevor killed those girls. Don't you just love the irony? Trevor stole my coins, not realizing what else I kept in that box. All my sweet things' jewelry. He didn't have a clue what he had. And now everyone believes he was the one who did those terrible things to those girls. It's too perfect."

"Not quite. Trevor and Arnie are dead. You can't blame this one on him or Arnie."

"I always get away with it," Pierce said, not sounding worried in the least. "I can make it look like you took off with her. Make sure someone uses your credit cards. I can keep the cops guessing for years until they tire of looking for the two of you."

Mac dropped his gaze to Jill. She motioned slowly with her head and his eyes followed the movement. She'd wrapped the rope loosely around Pierce's ankles as he'd been talking and now had the end, ready to pull it.

He gave only the slightest nod. She jerked the rope. At the same time, Mac drove his arm up, knocking the gun away. A shot exploded, echoing off the walls.

Pierce went down hard, his body kicking up dust from the floor as it hit. Mac dived for his weapon and was on Pierce before he could get up. He pressed the gun to the side of Pierce's head, and Pierce smiled up at him.

"You aren't going to kill me," he said. "It's not in you. And the bitch of it is, you know I can hire the best lawyer money can buy. I'll get off. Maybe a little time in a nice sanitarium. Then I'll be cured. I've gotten away with murder for years." The smile broadened. "I will again."

Mac could hear the coast guard boat nearing the island. "Yes, I know," he said to Pierce, and pulled the trigger.

Then he moved over to Jill.

Tears streaming down her cheeks, her eyes never leaving his face, she pulled Mac down and held him. He wrapped her in his arms.

"I knew you'd come back." Her words were a hoarse whisper coming from her injured throat.

He kept her wrapped in his arms as he watched the lights of the coast guard boat draw nearer and nearer.

Epilogue

Jill sat on the deck of her father's lake house and watched a sailboat move across the blue-green waters of Flathead Lake. She could smell the cherry blossoms on the slight breeze and hear her father and Darlene in the kitchen discussing their upcoming wedding.

Jill smiled at the thought of her father's happiness. It was matched only by her own. In the months since that horrible night at the Hillinger mansion, the memories had faded and blurred. Sometimes she still had nightmares but Mac was always there to hold her. She'd never felt safer. Or happier.

Mac had bought what Trevor had named Inspiration Island. He'd burned the old Hillinger mansion to the ground.

The remains of all the murdered young women had been removed and sent home for burial. At last their families could begin to heal. And Nathaniel Pierce was dead. He wouldn't hurt anyone ever again.

Jill turned at the sound of Mac's footfalls on the deck and smiled up at his handsome face. He stepped closer to her and she noticed he had one hand hidden behind his back.

"What?" she asked, laughing. Mac wasn't the kind of man who showered a woman with gifts. Thank goodness, she thought, remembering Trevor's.

"For you," Mac said shyly as he pulled the bouquet of wildflowers from behind his back.

Tears stung her eyes.

"I've never given flowers to a woman before," he said, dropping to his knees in front of her chair. "I wanted you to be the first."

She took the flowers, drawing him to her with her free arm. He kissed her neck and she felt that wonderful thrill she'd felt from the first.

And Mac *had* been wrong. When they'd made love again, it *was* more amazing than the first time. In fact, every time they made love was more amazing than the last.

Their spring wedding was huge and held at the church in Bigfork, overlooking the lake. The same church where Jill's father and Darlene would be married next week.

Mac had moved his P.I. business down from Whitefish and into a building he'd bought across the street from Jill's bakery. Zoe and Shane had moved into Jill's old apartment over the bakery, both of them working part-time while they attended junior college in Kalispell.

"I can't believe the change in Shane," Mac had said.

And Shane hadn't been able to believe the change in his uncle. "He's, like, human."

Mac had laughed and pulled his new bride to him.

They'd bought a place on the lake. From it, Jill couldn't see Inspiration Island. Mac said maybe someday they would build a camp on the island for kids. The island needed laughter. But first it needed to heal.

Alistair and Heddy Forester sold their house on the lake and moved away. Jill saw Alistair before he left. He looked like a very old man. He'd told her again how sorry he was. "I wish I could turn back the clock," he said, and shook his head, tears in his eyes.

"There is something we haven't talked about," Mac said now, drawing back from her.

She smiled at him. They'd talked for days after what had happened. Talked about his first wife, Emily. Her death. Mac's fear of loving again. His confession that he'd fallen for Jill that first night in the cottage.

They had taken it slowly, spending time together, talking about everything. That bond had been there from the beginning, though. It made it easy. It felt so right.

"What haven't we talked about?" she asked, looking from her bouquet of beautiful flowers to him. He'd put them in a small jar with water. The jar brimmed with the bright colors of spring. Like love, she thought.

"Kids," he said.

"Kids?" She thought he was talking about his

plan for the island. But then she looked into his eyes and felt a jolt. "Kids?" she repeated, her eyes filling with tears. She'd been so afraid he would never want children of their own. He'd taken the first step by letting himself love her completely, knowing he could lose her, just as he'd lost Emily, just as he'd almost lost Jill that night on the island.

Mac nodded. "Jill, I want to share this. I keep seeing you holding a baby in your arms. This love of ours, it's so strong...." He shook his head, at a loss for words.

He knew life could irreversibly change in an instant. Sometimes all it took was a kiss. His life had changed that night in the cottage when he'd kissed Jill Lawson. He couldn't explain it. But she was right, whatever had happened was more than sex. Sometimes two people connected in a way that tore down all barriers and united them forever.

She leaned forward, cupped his face in her hands and pressed a kiss to his mouth. "Say the words," she whispered against his lips.

He pulled back enough to look into her eyes and smiled. He had no idea what the future held. But he was no longer afraid. Losing was the flip side of loving. But loving was worth it. Whatever time he had with Jill, he intended to enjoy every moment of it. He was no longer afraid of making the same mistakes his father had made. He wasn't his father. And Jill Lawson was like no woman he'd ever met.

"I love you." The words came out so easily. "I love you." He lifted her into his arms and spun her around. "I love you! And I want a baby!"

She was laughing, a wondrous sound, and he was laughing, too, holding her and spinning, the world spinning around them, the two of them dizzy with happiness.

As he stopped and let her slowly slide down so he could kiss her again, he looked into her eyes, promising to give her love, all the love now bursting in his heart. He kissed her, and then they were spinning and laughing.

He heard Jill's father and Darlene come out onto the deck.

"What in the world?" her father said.

"We've decided to have a baby!" Jill announced.

"Babies," Mac said, and kissed her. "Lots of babies."

Life changed in an instant. His had changed with one kiss.

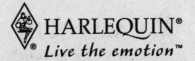

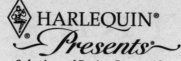

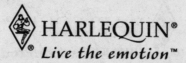

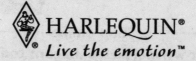

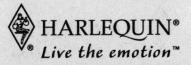

Three brothers, one tuxedo…and one destiny!

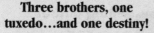
Date With Destiny

A brand-new anthology from
USA TODAY bestselling author

KRISTINE ROLOFSON
MURIEL JENSEN
KRISTIN GABRIEL

The package said "R. Perez" and inside was a tuxedo. But which Perez brother—Rick, Rafe or Rob—was it addressed to? This tuxedo is on a mission…to lead each of these men to the altar!

DATE WITH DESTINY will introduce you to the characters of *Forrester Square*… an exciting new continuity starting in August 2003.

Forrester Square
LEGACIES . LIES . LOVE .

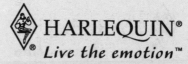

HARLEQUIN®
Live the emotion™

Visit us at www.eHarlequin.com

PHDWD

KATE WILHELM

SKELETONS

Lee Donne is an appendix in a family of overachievers. Her mother has three doctorates, her father is an economics genius and her grandfather is a world-renowned Shakespearean scholar. After four years of college and three majors, Lee is nowhere closer to a degree. With little better to do, she agrees to house-sit for her grandfather.

But the quiet stay she envisioned ends abruptly when she begins to hear strange noises at night. Something is hidden in the house…and someone is determined to find it. Suddenly Lee finds herself caught in a game of cat and mouse, the reasons for which she doesn't understand. But when the FBI arrives on the doorstep, she realizes that the house may hold dark secrets that go beyond her own family. And that sometimes, long-buried skeletons rise up from the grave.

"The mystery at the heart of this novel is well-crafted."
—*Publishers Weekly*

*Available the first week of July 2003
wherever paperbacks are sold!*

MIRA®

HARLEQUIN®
INTRIGUE®

presents another outstanding installment
in our bestselling series

COLORADO CONFIDENTIAL

By day these agents are cowboys; by night they are
specialized government operatives. Men bound by love,
loyalty and the law—they've vowed to keep their
missions and identities confidential...

August 2003
ROCKY MOUNTAIN MAVERICK
BY GAYLE WILSON

September 2003
SPECIAL AGENT NANNY
BY LINDA O. JOHNSTON

In **October,** look for an exciting short-story collection
featuring *USA TODAY* bestselling author
JASMINE CRESSWELL

November 2003
COVERT COWBOY
BY HARPER ALLEN

December 2003
A WARRIOR'S MISSION
BY RITA HERRON

PLUS
FIND OUT HOW IT ALL BEGAN
with three tie-in books from Harlequin Historicals,
starting January 2004

Available at your favorite retail outlet.

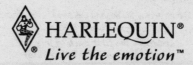

HARLEQUIN®
Live the emotion™